# A DESCRIPTIVE ATLAS

## of the

# PACIFIC ISLANDS

New Zealand, Australia, Polynesia, Melanesia, Micronesia, Philippines

*by*

T. F. KENNEDY

Maps by
JULIUS PETRO *and* LIONEL FORSDYKE

FREDERICK A. PRAEGER, *Publishers*
New York · Washington

## BOOKS THAT MATTER

Published in the United States of America in 1968
by Frederick A. Praeger, Inc., Publishers
111 Fourth Avenue, New York, N.Y. 10003

*This book was first published in 1966 in New Zealand by
A.H & A.W. Reed, Publishers. The present enlarged edition
has been thoroughly revised and brought up to date.*

Library of Congress Catalog Card Number: Map 68–9

Printed in New Zealand

# PREFACE

This atlas has been compiled because of the need to fill a gap in information about the Pacific. Too few maps exist of the many islands in the Pacific Ocean. Few of the islands are completely mapped, though work is progressing steadily in several groups.

Until now there has been no atlas which brings together maps of all the main island groups and of the more important individual islands. The present atlas has been designed primarily for use in schools in the Pacific Islands and in surrounding countries. It should also prove useful to people living in the Pacific area, to tourists, and to all who have an interest in the Pacific.

The descriptive material has been kept to a factual account and makes no claim to be exhaustive. The same headings have been used in the texts relating to each island group so that comparisons can be easily made. So far as possible, the latest available statistics have been included. These are often official estimates.

The arrangement of the maps into sections on New Zealand, Australia, Polynesia, Melanesia, Micronesia, and the Philippines is purely one of convenience. Emphasis has been placed on the economically more important islands and those of particular interest to New Zealand and Australia.

The task of compilation has not been an easy one because of the scarcity of suitable maps and the difficulty of obtaining up-to-date cartographical information about all the islands. It is hoped, however, that the atlas will do much to increase knowledge of the insular Pacific world.

T.F.K.

# PREFACE TO REVISED EDITION

The most recent statistics available have been included and several minor corrections made to the text. The sections on Government in Fiji, Nauru, and in the British Solomon Islands have been brought up to date.

It should be noted that Australia, New Guinea, New Zealand, Cook Islands, Nuie, Tonga, W. Samoa, Tokelaus, and Gilbert and Ellice Islands have recently converted to decimal currency; the dollar unit being equal to half the previous £ unit.

T.F.K.

# CONTENTS

# ACKNOWLEDGMENTS

The idea for the atlas was first suggested by Mr F. R. J. Davies, Officer for Islands Education, New Zealand Education Department, who has subsequently given advice and help. It is not possible to acknowledge the many other people who have assisted with material, but Island officials and Island Surveys Departments have contributed generously, and officers of the New Zealand Lands and Survey Department, the New Zealand Meteorological Service, the New Zealand Department of Island Territories and the New Zealand Soil Bureau have been most helpful. A number of people, including Mr J. M. McEwen, Secretary for Maori Affairs, formerly Secretary of Island Territories, who know the Islands well, have been kind enough to read and to advise on the material.

Especial thanks are due to Mr J. Petro for his skill and care in drawing the maps, to Mr L. Forsdyke who assisted him, and to Mr D. W. Sinclair for his patience, technical advice, and co-ordination of the project.

T.F.K.

# LIST OF MAPS

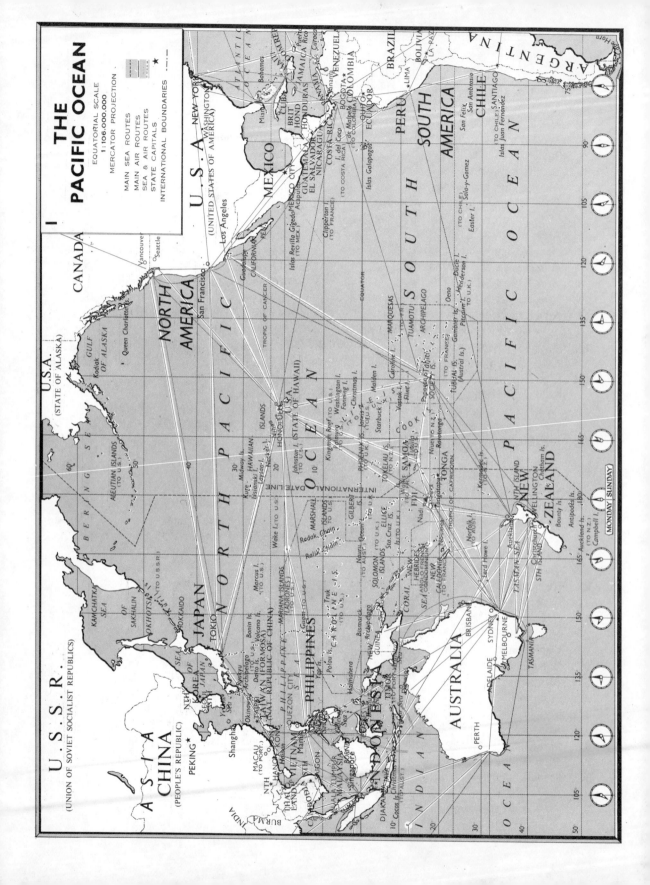

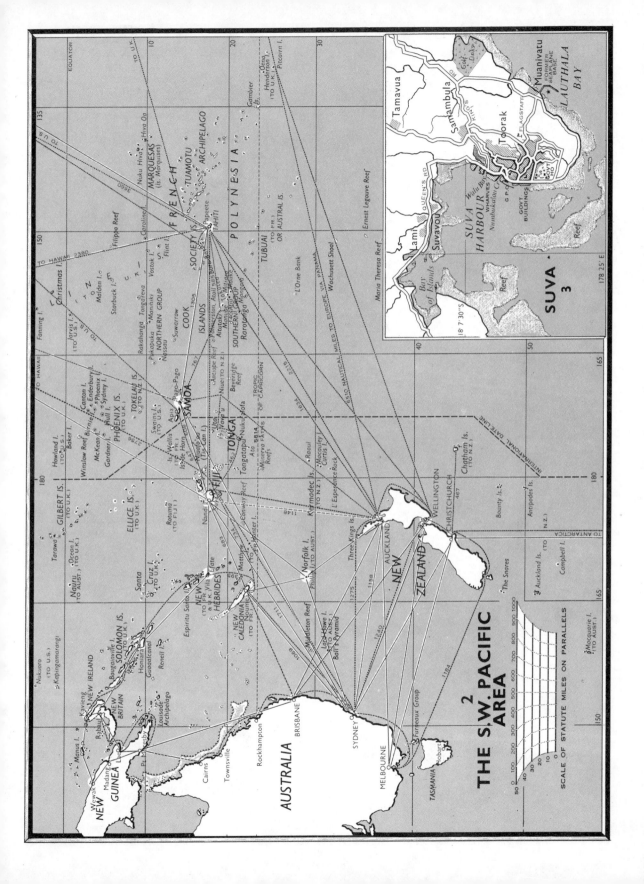

THE S.W. PACIFIC
AREA

2

SCALE OF STATUTE MILES ON PARALLELS

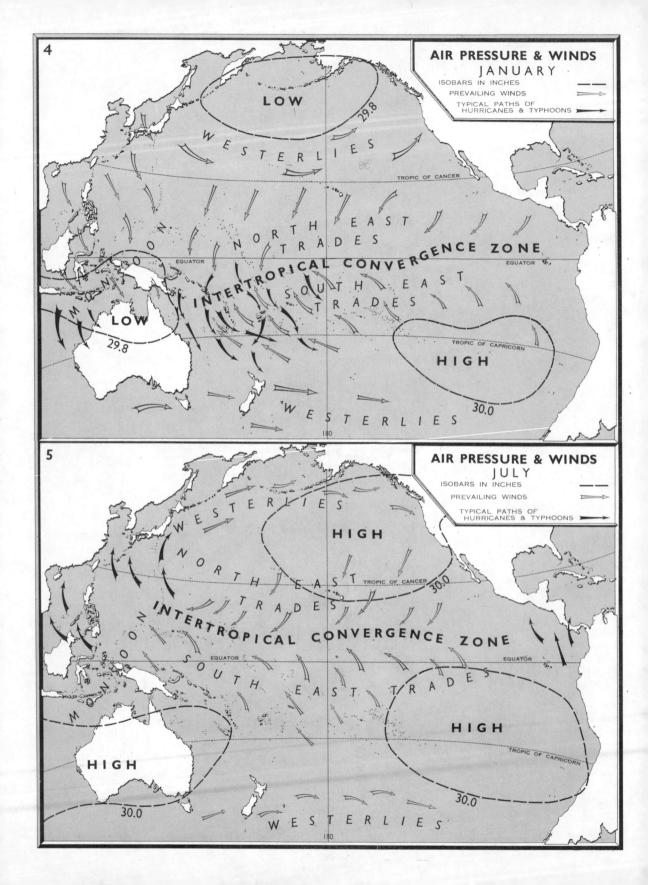

**4**

AIR PRESSURE & WINDS
JANUARY
ISOBARS IN INCHES
PREVAILING WINDS
TYPICAL PATHS OF
HURRICANES & TYPHOONS

LOW

29.8

W E S T E R L I E S

TROPIC OF CANCER

N O R T H   E A S T   T R A D E S

EQUATOR                                          EQUATOR

INTERTROPICAL CONVERGENCE ZONE

S O U T H   E A S T   T R A D E S

LOW

29.8

TROPIC OF CAPRICORN

HIGH

30.0

W E S T E R L I E S

180

**5**

AIR PRESSURE & WINDS
JULY
ISOBARS IN INCHES
PREVAILING WINDS
TYPICAL PATHS OF
HURRICANES & TYPHOONS

W E S T E R L I E S

HIGH

N O R T H   E A S T   TROPIC OF CANCER   30.0

T R A D E S

INTERTROPICAL CONVERGENCE ZONE

EQUATOR                                          EQUATOR

S O U T H   E A S T   T R A D E S

HIGH

TROPIC OF CAPRICORN

30.0

HIGH

30.0

W E S T E R L I E S

180

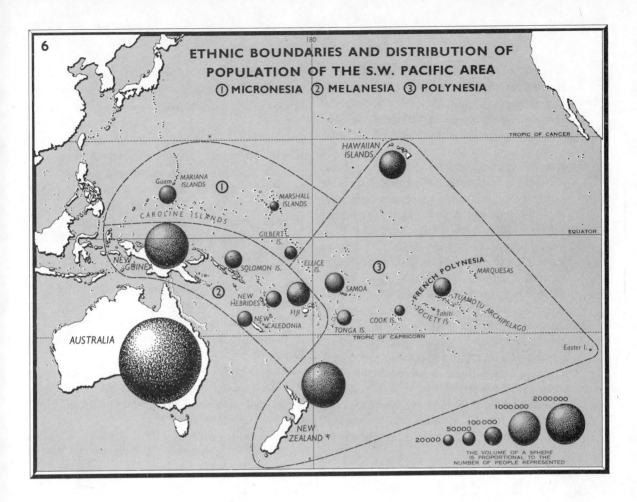

**ETHNIC BOUNDARIES AND DISTRIBUTION OF
POPULATION OF THE S.W. PACIFIC AREA**
① MICRONESIA ② MELANESIA ③ POLYNESIA

TROPIC OF CANCER

HAWAIIAN
ISLANDS

Guam  MARIANA
ISLANDS  ①

MARSHALL
ISLANDS

CAROLINE ISLANDS

EQUATOR

GILBERT
IS.

NEW
GUINEA

SOLOMON IS.

ELLICE
IS.

③

FRENCH POLYNESIA

MARQUESAS

②

NEW
HEBRIDES

SAMOA

TUAMOTU ARCHIPELAGO

FIJI

NEW
CALEDONIA

COOK IS.

Tahiti

SOCIETY IS.

TONGA IS.

TROPIC OF CAPRICORN

Easter I.

AUSTRALIA

NEW
ZEALAND

2000000

1000000

100000

50000

20000

THE VOLUME OF A SPHERE
IS PROPORTIONAL TO THE
NUMBER OF PEOPLE REPRESENTED

# THE PACIFIC AREA

**Structure:** The Pacific Ocean covers almost one third of the surface of the earth. It occupies a large, saucer-like, structural depression. The surrounding rim is mountainous and volcanic. The ocean floor of the central Pacific is uniform, with depths usually of 10,000 ft to 15,000 ft. The western part of the floor consists of mountain arcs and deep trenches (e.g. Philippines Trench, 37,782 ft; Tonga Trench, 35,000 ft). Many of the mountain arcs rise above the sea as island groups (e.g. Solomon Islands, New Zealand). Islands are more numerous in the western part of the ocean.

The island types fall into "high" islands and "low" islands. The former may be (a) of non-volcanic rocks with some volcanic material (e.g. the mountain arc islands), or (b) volcanic mountains (e.g. Hawaii, Rarotonga). "High" islands are often surrounded by coral reefs.

The "low" islands are of coral formation, usually built on top of undersea mountains, and they may be atolls (low, palm-covered islets enclosing a lagoon, e.g. Tarawa), or raised coral islands (e.g. Nauru Island, Vavau Island).

**Climate:** Because of its huge area, there are naturally wide differences in Pacific climates.

9

The two maps on page 8 show the main factors influencing general climate. In northerly and in southerly latitudes there are marked seasonal differences in temperature and weather is controlled by mid-latitude anticyclones and the westerly air stream. In the tropical Pacific, where most of the islands lie, there is reasonable uniformity. Except on larger or higher islands, temperatures vary little throughout the year, registering mainly between 70°F and 80°F. Here the trade winds dominate. Blowing steadily, they bring more rain to the windward sides of "high" islands. Leeward sides and "low" islands often have low rainfalls, and droughts are common during the "dry" or "low sun" season. Where the trade winds meet is the inter-tropical convergence zone. This moves north and south with the seasons (see maps), and rain frequently develops in this zone.

In the far western Pacific winds are influenced by the huge land masses of Asia and Australia, which produce a "monsoon" effect (see map). Tropical cyclones (typhoons, hurricanes) occur particularly in the west and south-west Pacific. These violent storms often cause considerable damage.

**People:** The divisions of Polynesia (many islands), Melanesia (islands of dark-skinned people), and Micronesia (small islands) are based on the kinds of people who first inhabited these areas. Polynesians are brown-skinned people of dominantly Caucasoid features. Melanesians are dark-skinned, with Negritoid and Australoid features and with frizzy hair. Micronesians are brown-skinned, have a mongoloid strain, and are shorter in stature than Melanesians.

During the last 150 years large numbers of people from countries outside the Pacific Ocean or on its borders have settled in the various islands. People from Europe and Asia have added their cultures to the Pacific world and in several areas are now dominant in numbers (e.g. Hawaii, Fiji, New Zealand, New Caledonia).

# NEW ZEALAND

**Size and Physical Nature:** Area 103,736 sq. miles. Consists of North Island, South Island, Stewart Island and numerous offshore islands.

The country is hilly and mountainous. A main mountain axis, running from Fiordland in the S.W. of the South Island to East Cape in the North Island, divides the islands into eastern and western regions. These mountains, rising to Mt Cook (12,349 ft) in the Southern Alps, are important as rain-water collecting areas for lakes and rivers. Relatively small areas of flat land occur on either side of the mountains. These lowlands are mainly discontinuous coastal plains and river valleys (see map). Other areas of fairly flat land occur as high inland basins and plateaux (e.g.

Mackenzie Basin, and the Volcanic Plateau). In the Southern Alps many glaciers flow from snow and icefields.

The North Island has much evidence of volcanic activity, including the volcanoes of Tongariro National Park (Mts Ruapehu, 9,175 ft; Ngauruhoe, active; and Tongariro), Mt Egmont in Taranaki, and many other smaller volcanic cones in the Rotorua area, Waikato, Auckland, and Northland.

**Government:** New Zealand is a self-governing state and a member of the British Commonwealth. Queen Elizabeth II, the reigning head, is represented by a Governor-General. Parliament consists of 76 European and four Maori elected members working on the party system.

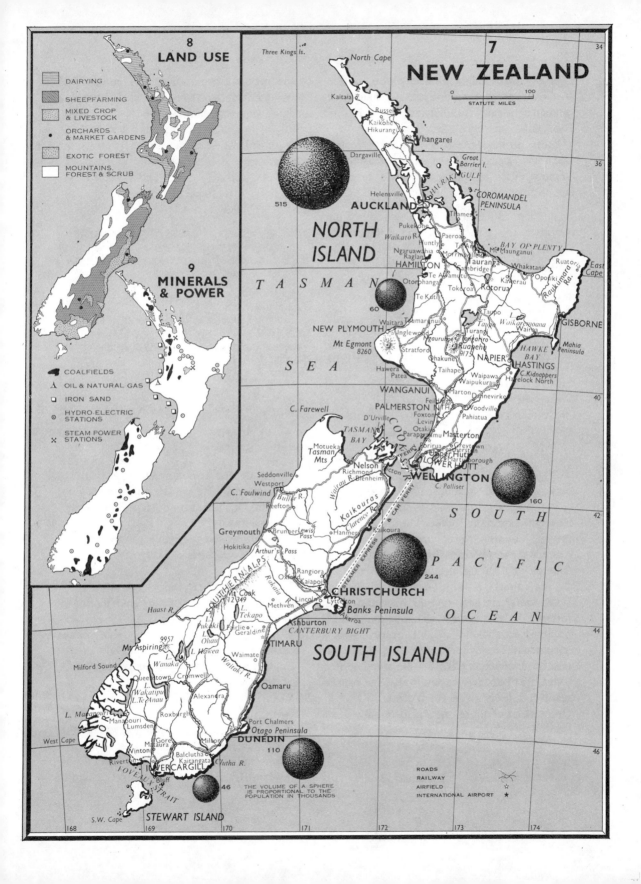

# 8
## LAND USE

DAIRYING
SHEEPFARMING
MIXED CROP & LIVESTOCK
ORCHARDS & MARKET GARDENS
EXOTIC FOREST
MOUNTAINS, FOREST & SCRUB

# 9
## MINERALS & POWER

COALFIELDS
OIL & NATURAL GAS
IRON SAND
HYDRO-ELECTRIC STATIONS
STEAM POWER STATIONS

# 7
# NEW ZEALAND

0                    100
STATUTE MILES

Three Kings Is.
North Cape
Kaitaia
Russell
Kaikohe
Hikurangi
Whangarei
Dargaville
Great Barrier I.
HAURAKI GULF
Helensville
COROMANDEL PENINSULA
AUCKLAND
Thames
NORTH ISLAND
Pukekohe
Paeroa
Waikato R.
Huntly
Te Aroha
BAY OF PLENTY
Ngaruawahia
Te Puke
Mt Maunganui
Raglan
Tauranga
Whakatane
HAMILTON
Cambridge
Kawerau
Opotiki
Ruatoria
East Cape
Te Awamutu
Rotorua
Raukumara Ra.
Otorohanga
Kaiwera
Te Kuiti
Taupo
Waikaremoana
GISBORNE
515
60
Taumarunui
L. Taupo
Waitara
New Plymouth
Inglewood
Ngauruhoe
Tongariro
Turangi
Wairoa
Mt Egmont 8260
Stratford
Ruapehu 9175
NAPIER
Mahia Peninsula
HAWKE BAY
Ohakune
HASTINGS
Taihape
Havelock North
Hawera
C. Kidnappers
Patea
Waipawa
Waipukurau
WANGANUI
Marton
Dannevirke
TASMAN SEA
Feilding
PALMERSTON NTH
Woodville
Foxton
Pahiatua
C. Farewell
D'Urville I.
Levin
Otaki
TASMAN BAY
Paraparaumu
Masterton
Motueka
Porirua
Greytown
Tasman Mts
Carterton
Upper Hutt
Nelson
Martinborough
Richmond
Picton
LOWER HUTT
160
Seddonville
Wairau R.
Blenheim
WELLINGTON
Westport
C. Palliser
C. Foulwind
Kaikouras
COOK STRAIT
Reefton
Clarence R.
Greymouth
Brunner
Lewis Pass
Hanmer
Kaikoura
SOUTH
Hokitika
Arthur's Pass
244
PACIFIC
SOUTHERN ALPS
Rangiora
Oxford
Mt Cook 12349
Rakaia R.
Kaiapoi
Haast R.
L. Tekapo
Methven
Lincoln
CHRISTCHURCH
L. Pukaki
Lyttelton
OCEAN
Fairlie
Banks Peninsula
Mt Aspiring 9957
L. Ohau
Akaroa
L. Hawea
Geraldine
Ashburton
Milford Sound
L. Wanaka
Waimate
CANTERBURY BIGHT
TIMARU
Queenstown
Cromwell
SOUTH ISLAND
L. Wakatipu
Oamaru
L. Te Anau
Alexandra
L. Manapouri
Roxburgh
Manapouri
Lumsden
Port Chalmers
West Cape
Mataura
Gore
Otago Peninsula
Winton
Milton
DUNEDIN
Riverton
Balclutha
110
INVERCARGILL
Kaitangata
Clutha R.
Bluff
46
FOVEAUX STRAIT
THE VOLUME OF A SPHERE IS PROPORTIONAL TO THE POPULATION IN THOUSANDS
S.W. Cape
STEWART ISLAND

ROADS
RAILWAY
AIRFIELD
INTERNATIONAL AIRPORT

168   169   170   171   172   173   174

34
36
40
42
44
46

Cabinet consists of 16 ministers who control 44 Government departments. An Executive Council consists of Cabinet and the Governor-General.

Local government is important. Elected Local Bodies control the administration of counties, cities, education, hospitals, roading, etc.

**Population and Settlement:** The indigenous people are Maoris, who are Polynesians. European settlement began about 1830. The Europeans are mainly of British stock. Chinese, Indians, Pacific Islanders, Lebanese, and Syrians comprise about one per cent of the population.

More than two-thirds of the people live in the North Island, and there is a drift of population from south to north. About two-thirds of the people live in towns and cities. The remainder live chiefly on dispersed farms or in small country centres. Houses are built mainly of timber, with some of brick, and all are supplied with electric power. There is an extensive system of schools and universities. Education is free, secular, and compulsory.

### Population

| Date | Total | Maoris |
|------|-------|--------|
| 1861 | 99,021 | |
| 1901 | 772,719 | 43,143 |
| 1921 | 1,218,913 | 52,751 |
| 1956 | 2,174,062 | 137,151 |
| 1966 | 2,676,919 | 198,188 |

Density of Population 25 per sq. mile
Rate of increase 2.1%
Birth Rate: (European) 21 per 1,000; (Maori) 40 per 1,000
Death Rate: (European) 9 per 1,000; (Maori) 6 per 1,000

**Climate and Vegetation:**

| | Auckland | Hokitika | Dunedin |
|---|---|---|---|
| Average annual rainfall | 49″ | 109″ | 31″ |
| Average temperature (January) | 66.5°F | 58.5°F | 59.5°F |
| Average temperature (July) | 51.5°F | 44.5°F | 43.5°F |

Rainfall over most of the country is between 25″ and 60″ and is adequate for plant growth. Winters are mild though frosts are frequent, especially in the South Island and the hill country. Snow occurs in the high country in winter. Prevailing winds are from the west and rainfall is higher on the west of the mountains.

Originally most of New Zealand was forested. Extensive areas of tussock grassland occurred in the east of the South Island. Much of the east and central North Island was scrub covered. Clearing has reduced the forest area but large exotic forests have been planted, especially on the Volcanic Plateau. One quarter of the country is forested.

### Forest Area

| | |
|---|---|
| Native trees | 16,000,000 acres |
| Exotic trees | 850,000 acres |

**Land Tenure and Farming:** One third of the land is owned by individuals and this may be freely sold. One sixteenth is Maori land, some three-elevenths is Crown land, about one quarter is reserved for public purposes, and the remainder consists of lakes, rivers, roads, etc.

Forty-four million acres are used for farming, which comprises the following main types (see map on page 11):

1. Extensive pastoral farming (sheep and cattle) on native pasture – mainly in the South Island. Farms are many thousands of acres in size.
2. Extensive pastoral farming (sheep and cattle) on sown hill country – mainly in the North Island. Farms average about 2,000 acres in size.
3. Intensive pastoral farming (for dairying or fat lambs) on fertile flat to rolling land.

Farms range from about 50 to 1,000 acres in size.

4. Arable farming – crops (such as wheat, oats, barley, potatoes), and often fat lambs. Mainly in the eastern South Island.

5. Orchards, market gardens, and poultry farms.

New Zealand soils are not naturally fertile and require dressings of lime and phosphates in particular.

Only 15 per cent of the working population work on farms.

### Area in Grain Crops
437,000 acres (60% in Canterbury)

### No. of Livestock

|  | 1964 | 1966 |
|---|---|---|
| Sheep | 51,292,000 | 57,340,000 |
| Dairy Cattle | 3,128,000 | 3,353,000 |
| Beef Cattle | 3,568,000 | 3,816,000 |
| Pigs | 771,000 | 653,500 |

**Exports:** **1966**
Total £375 million

| Wool | £115.7 | million |
|---|---|---|
| Meat | £97.5 | million |
| Dairy Produce | £86.7 | million |
| Pulp and Paper and Timber | £12.4 | million |

(£NZ1 = $NZ2)

**Industry:** Primary industry is concerned with the milling of forests, mining coal, iron sand and natural gas, quarrying, fishing, and the generation of hydro-electric and geothermal power.

Manufacturing, other than the processing of primary produce, has developed mostly since World War II. Many factories are small, over half employing fewer than ten workers. Food manufacturing, which includes meat freezing, butter and cheese making, vegetable canning, flour milling, etc., is the most important. Other manufacturing includes textiles and clothing, paper, fertilisers, machinery, transport supplies, and household appliances.

The main factory centres are Auckland, Wellington-Lower Hutt, Christchurch, Dunedin, Hamilton, Rotorua, Palmerston North, and Invercargill.

**Cities and Towns:** Wellington is the capital city, but Auckland has the largest population, greatest manufacturing and commercial activities, and the busiest port. Auckland is growing more rapidly than any other city. The main centres, with their populations, are:

|  | 1965 | 1966 |
|---|---|---|
| Urban Auckland | 515,100 | 547,915 |
| Hamilton | 59,900 | 63,327 |
| Napier | 37,100 | 39,095 |
| New Plymouth | 35,300 | 35,762 |
| Palmerston North | 48,500 | 49,237 |
| Wellington | 161,600 | 167,844 |
| Lower Hutt | 111,400 | 114,739 |
| Christchurch | 243,900 | 246,773 |
| Dunedin | 109,300 | 108,680 |
| Invercargill | 46,390 | 45,973 |

In addition, there are many small towns situated in areas of farming, mining, and tourism.

**Communications:** Regular overseas and coastal steamship services call at all the main ports. Auckland and Christchurch have international airports. There is an extensive internal system of airways, railways, roads, radio and television networks, and daily newspapers.

# AUSTRALIA

**Size and Physical Nature:** Area 2,974,581 sq. miles. Twenty-nine times as large as New Zealand. Consists of the continent of Australia, the island of Tasmania, and numerous offshore islands.

The country can be divided broadly into (a) the East Australian Highlands, an area of low mountains (Mt Kosciusko, 7,328 ft, is the highest), broken plateaux, valleys, and coastal plains; (b) a series of low, interior, sedimentary basins, mostly below 500 ft (Lake Eyre is below sea level); (c) the Western Plateau, a shield of ancient rocks, occupying some three-fifths of the country and consisting of vast deserts, savannah, scattered rocky mountain ranges, and rock outcrops.

The northern half of Australia lies within the tropics and in the area of coral growth. The Great Barrier Reef off the Queensland coast is the largest coral reef in the world.

**Government:** The Commonwealth of Australia is a Federation of six states, each of which has its own Parliament, Premier, and Governor. The Governors represent the reigning head, Queen Elizabeth II, in the six State Parliaments, while a Governor-General represents the Queen in the Federal Parliament. The Federal Parliament, located in Canberra, consists of the Governor-General, the Senate of 60 members (in which the states have equal elected representation), and the House of Representatives with 124 members (in which the states are represented by elected members, in proportion to their population). The Australian Capital Territory, which includes Canberra, and the Northern Territory are directly administered by the Australian Government.

**Population and Settlement:** The indigenous people are aborigines who now number about 40,000. European settlement began in 1788. The people are chiefly of British stock. There have been over a million immigrants from various parts of Britain and Europe since the Second World War. There are some 20,000 Chinese and Indians and 20,000 of other races.

### Population

| Date | Total |
|------|-------|
| 1881 | 2,250,194 |
| 1901 | 3,773,801 |
| 1921 | 5,435,734 |
| 1954 | 8,986,873 |
| 1966 | 11,540,764 |

Density of Population 4 per sq. mile
Rate of Increase 2.01%
Birth Rate 19 per 1,000
Death Rate 8.2 per 1,000

Four-fifths of the people live in the S.E. corner of Australia (from just north of Brisbane to just west of Adelaide). About four-fifths of the total population live in towns and cities; the remainder on dispersed farms and small mining and fishing settlements. Houses are of wood, brick, or concrete and are well served with power and water.

There is an extensive system of schools, universities, and medical services. Isolated "outback" farms and settlements are served by a unique "school of the air" and a "Royal Flying Doctor" service.

**Climate and Vegetation:**

|  | Sydney | Darwin | Perth | Alice Springs |
|---|--------|--------|-------|---------------|
| Average annual rainfall | 45" | 62" | 36" | 11" |
| Average temperature (January) | 72°F | 86°F | 74°F | 95°F |
| Average temperature (July) | 54°F | 77°F | 55°F | 40°F |

The distribution of rain has a concentric pattern, increasing from the desert centre outwards. Apart from the northern peninsulas and S.W. Australia, only Eastern Australia has over 25" per year. Southern Australia has rain in the winter months, tropical Northern Australia in the summer from the monsoon. Eastern Australia has rain all year. Snow falls in winter in the southern part of the Eastern Highlands or Australian Alps.

The vegetation pattern follows the rainfall. Forests of eucalypts (in the east) and hardwoods (in the west) occur in the higher rainfall areas, with some tropical rain-forest in the north and north-east. These grade away inland through savannah and grassland to desert.

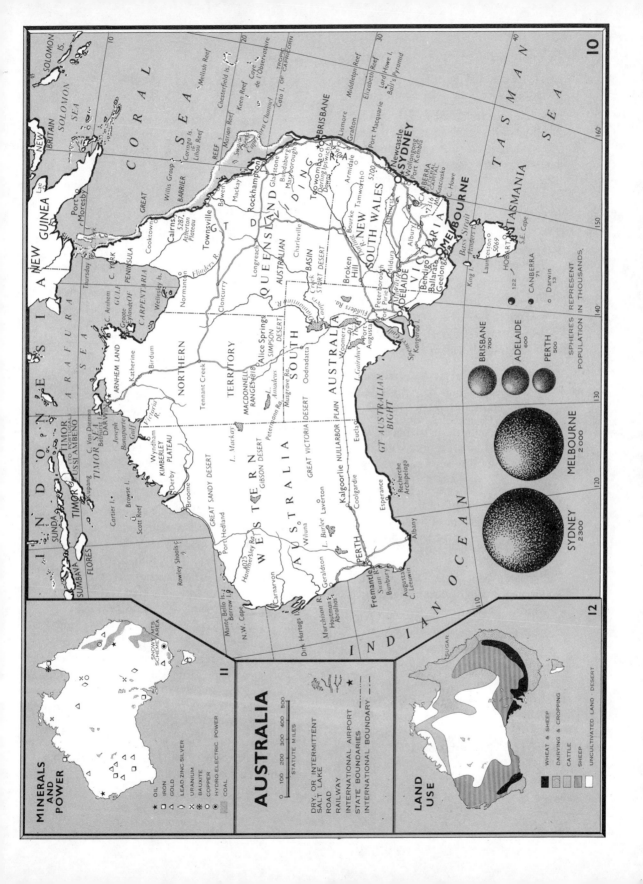

**Land Tenure and Farming:** Land is owned individually or leased from the state. Considerable areas are reserved for public use and as water catchments, etc.

**Main types of Farming are:**

1. Extensive sheep farming on native grasses of the inlands. Farms are up to 200,000 acres in size.

2. Sheep and wheat farming, in the 13″ to 25″ rainfall areas. Farms average from 500 to 3,000 acres.

3. Extensive cattle farming in Queensland, Northern Territory, and Western Australia. Farms (stations) are hundreds of square miles in extent.

4. Intensive pastoral farming (fattening sheep or beef cattle, and dairying). Mainly on the east coast and in the south-west.

5. Arable farming – particularly wheat on large farms in areas receiving 10″ to 25″ of rain, but also oats, barley, hay, maize, potatoes, and vegetables.

6. Tropical farming. Sugar cane, pineapples, bananas, and tropical fruits in Queensland and Northern Territory. Cotton and rice in the Northern Territory.

7. Orchards, vineyards, etc., particularly in Tasmania and, under irrigation, in the Murray Basin.

Low rainfall, droughts, and lack of water for irrigation severely limit extension of both livestock and arable farming.

Several artesian basins, which provide underground water, are of tremendous importance to farming in the drier areas.

### No. of Stock (1966)

| Sheep | Cattle | Pigs |
|---|---|---|
| 158,000,000 | 18,000,000 | 1,746,000 |

### Area in Crops (1965)

| | |
|---|---|
| Cereals | 24,000,000 acres* |
| Sugar Cane | 647,000 acres |
| Cotton | 56,000 acres |
| Vegetables | 290,000 acres |
| Vineyards | 140,000 acres |
| Fruit | 315,000 acres |

*Wheat 71%

### Main Exports:    1965-6

| | |
|---|---|
| Agricultural Produce | $553 million* |
| Meat and Wool | $1,074 million |
| Dairy Produce | $83 million |
| Forestry | $11 million |
| Fish | $25 million |
| Minerals and Metal manufactures | $560 million |
| Gold | $24 million |

Total Exports $2,721 million

*Wheat $264 million

**Industry:** Australia has very substantial industrial resources. Power from coal, hydro-electricity (especially the Snowy River scheme), natural gas and petroleum, and a wide variety of mineral deposits, including iron ore, copper, lead, silver, zinc, bauxite, tin, gold, asbestos, ilmenite, sulphur, and uranium. As a result, large modern industries are concerned with steel making, metallurgy, machines, heavy chemicals, the manufacture of motor vehicles, and shipbuilding.

Other important industries are pulp and paper, rubber manufacturing, textiles and clothing, radio and electrical equipment, brewing, tobacco processing, printing, and many others. Factories concerned with the processing of meat, dairy produce, wheat-flour, sugar cane, fruit and vegetables, and the manufacture of foodstuffs, are widely distributed. The bulk (four-fifths) of industrial activity is located in the south-east corner of the country.

Thirty per cent of workers are engaged in mining and manufacturing.

**Cities and Towns:** The main centres with their populations (1964) are:

| | |
|---|---|
| Sydney | 2,300,100 |
| Melbourne | 2,061,300 |
| Brisbane | 663,500 |
| Adelaide | 607,800 |
| Perth | 457,000 |
| Hobart | 122,950 |
| Canberra | 77,644 |
| Darwin | 15,218 |

Canberra is the Federal capital of Australia but Sydney is the largest city, followed by Melbourne.

There are many other centres; in the country, in mining areas, and at resorts.

**Communications:** Regular passenger and cargo ships call at all the main ports. International airlines connect the main cities with the rest of the world. Internal communications, by rail and road, are excellent in the more closely settled east and south-west. Over the rest of the country, surface travel is often difficult and roads are few, though these are being extended for stock transport. Only one road crosses the country from north to south. On this account internal airways are rapidly increasing in importance.

Television and radio services are well developed, as is the publication of newspapers, magazines and books.

**Special Features:**
1. Australia's native animal population is unique. Nearly half of the 250 species of native mammals are marsupials.
2. Australia changed to dollar currency in 1966. £A1 = $A2.

# WESTERN SAMOA

**Size and Physical Nature:** Area 1,133 sq. miles, consisting of two large islands, Upolu (430 sq. miles) and Savai'i (703 sq. miles), together with the very small islands of Apolima, Manono, Fanuatapu, Namua, Nuutele, Nuulua, and Nuusafee.

The islands are mountainous and volcanic, rising to 6,094 ft in Savai'i and to 3,608 ft in Upolu. Inland hill slopes are steep. Much of the surface of the islands is covered with lava flows or is littered with black scoria rocks. Because of steep slopes and rock-strewn soil, less than half the area is suitable for farming development.

**Government:** Western Samoa is an independent state, having achieved independence on 1 January 1962.

It was administered by Germany until World War I; by New Zealand under mandate of the League of Nations until World War II; and then by New Zealand, but as a United Nations Trusteeship Territory, until 1961. Each village has a council of *matai* or heads of families. (A family consists of, usually, 20 or more people related by blood.)

**Population and Settlement:** Samoans are Polynesians. Ninety per cent of the population is full Polynesian.

### Population

| Date | Samoans | Euronesians | Europeans and others | Total |
|---|---|---|---|---|
| 1930 | 40,722 | 2,269 | 835 | 43,826 |
| 1943 | 60,957 | 3,027 | 280 | 64,264 |
| 1956 | 94,665 | 7,900 | 662 | 103,227 |
| 1961 | 101,288 | 11,813 | 1,326 | 114,427 (census) |
| 1966 | .. | .. | .. | 131,552 (census) |

### Population of Islands (1966)

| | |
|---|---:|
| Upolu (including Manono and Apolima) | 95,344 |
| Savai'i | 36,208 |

Birth Rate 33 per 1,000
Death Rate 5.6 per 1,000

Rate of population increase (3.8 per cent) is one of the highest in the world. Population density is 116 per sq. mile of total land but 920 per sq. mile of cultivated land.

Samoans live in villages averaging in size 400-500 people. The villages are situated along the coast with easy access to shore, reef, and sea fishing. Houses are oval, with open sides and thatched roof, set on platforms of scoria boulders. Churches and schools are important in village life. Unlike other islands, water in many areas is piped as well as being drawn from rain tanks, streams and springs.

**Climate and Vegetation:** Rainfall increases with altitude (113" at Apia; 250" at 3,000 ft), and is greater on south and east coasts because of the effect of mountain ranges on the S.E. trade winds (Lotofaga 160"). May to October is a "drier" season than the remainder of the year. Hurricanes occur.

Temperatures are fairly uniform, averaging 78°F to 80°F at sea level but falling to 63°F to 65°F at 4,000 ft.

The hot, wet, humid climate encourages luxuriant plant growth. Apart from village areas, cultivations, and recent lava flows, Samoa is densely forested. Coastal strips and lower slopes are in coconuts and small bush.

**Land Tenure and Farming:** Europeans and missions own five per cent of the total land. All other land is owned by Samoans or by the Crown, though some is leased by Europeans. Of the 105,000 acres at present in cultivation, about four-fifths is farmed by villagers.

By custom ownership of land lies in the family group. The *matai* or family head has the responsibility of administering the land for the benefit of the whole family group.

Each *matai* holds the right to portions of the land near the village. This right can be extended simply by clearing a new piece of land.

Farming is carried out on a family basis. The men go out on several days a week to plant or harvest taro, sweet potato, manioc, bananas, and cocoa, using hand tools. Plots may be scattered, with a tangle of coconuts and bush between them.

Half the cultivated land is in coconuts. Village families produce 80 per cent of Western Samoa's copra.

**Exports:**

**1961**

| | | |
|---|---|---:|
| Copra | 13,100 tons | £672,900 |
| Bananas | 560,442 cases | £664,500 |
| Cocoa | 4,200 tons | £597,600 |
| Other | | £11,500 |
| | Total | £1,946,500 |

**1965**

| | | |
|---|---|---:|
| Copra | 12,370 tons | £839,138 |
| Bananas | 481,565 cases | £609,873 |
| Cocoa | 2,841 tons | £450,450 |
| Others | | £140,550 |
| | Total | £2,040,011 |

**Towns:** Apia (25,000) is the capital and only large town. It is the only overseas port but the harbour is not a good one, being exposed to northerly winds and swell. The main street parallels the waterfront. A deep-water harbour is being developed at Asau in Savai'i.

**Communications:** Regular twice-monthly steamers from New Zealand, Fiji, and Tonga call at Apia with mail, passengers, and cargo. They load bananas and other cargo for Fiji and New Zealand. Transpacific cargo vessels call fairly frequently and copra boats call from time to time.

Several small craft ply between Apia and Pago-Pago in American Samoa and there is a regular launch service between Upolu and Savai'i.

Faleolo airport on Upolu provides for air services from Fiji and American Samoa.

Apia has a broadcasting station and can receive TV from Pago-Pago.

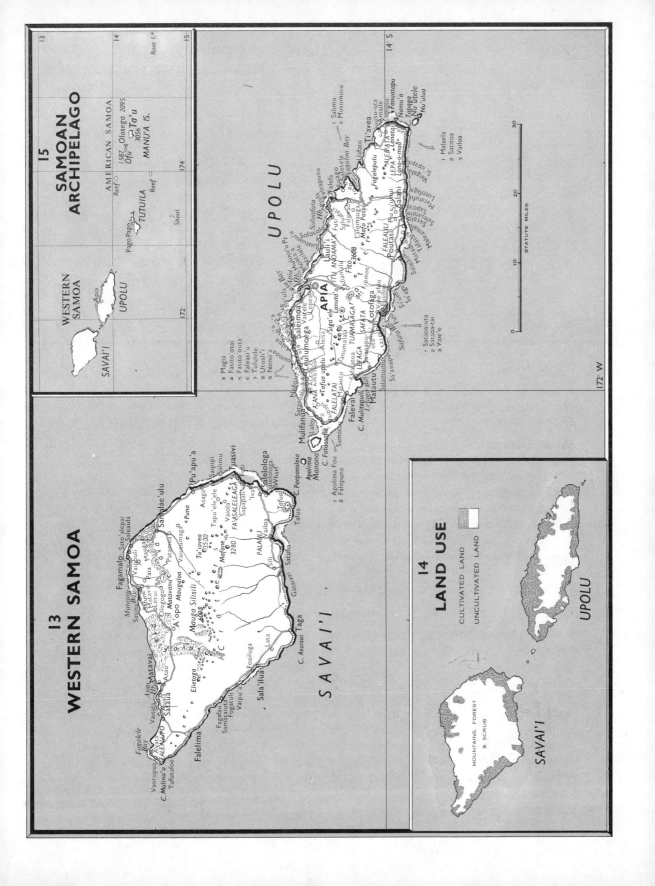

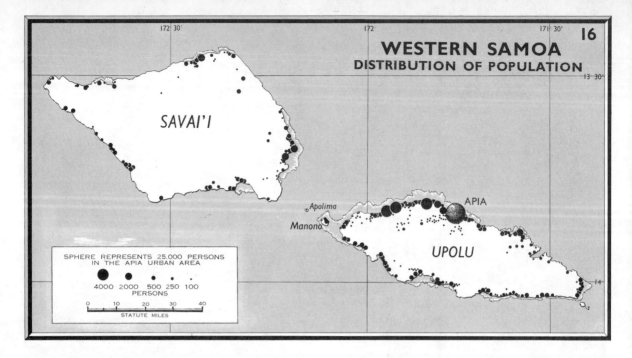

**WESTERN SAMOA**
DISTRIBUTION OF POPULATION

SAVAI'I

Apolima

Manono

APIA

UPOLU

SPHERE REPRESENTS 25,000 PERSONS
IN THE APIA URBAN AREA

4000  2000  500  250  100
PERSONS

0    10    20    30    40
STATUTE MILES

**Industry:** Apart from sawmills, local industry consists of building and maintenance, and consumer industries such as a soap factory, aerated waters, bakeries, etc.

**Special Features:**

1. The Observatory at Apia, founded in 1902, makes an important contribution to geophysical studies.

2. The tomb of Robert Louis Stevenson on Mt Vaea commemorates his life and work.

3. The islands are infested with the rhinoceros beetle, a serious pest of coconuts. Bananas are affected by Bunchy Top, a serious virus disease.

4. Western Samoa is famous for the architectural variety and magnificence of the churches.

5. There is a marked movement of people from rural districts to Apia.

6. Samoans have retained much of their traditional way of life in spite of exposure to Western influences.

7. Because of the rocky composition of the soil mechanical cultivation is impracticable.

# EASTERN SAMOA
## (American Samoa)

**Size and Physical Nature:** Consists of seven islands (76 sq. miles): Tutuila (42 sq. miles) and Aunu'u (1 sq. mile); Ta'u (17 sq. miles), Olosega, and Ofu in the Manu'a group; and Rose Island and Swains Island, which are two coral atolls. The main islands are of volcanic origin. Tutuila has a mountain range along its length and is nearly bisected by the beautiful harbour of Pago-Pago bay.

Eastern Samoa is an unincorporated territory of the United States administered by the Department of the Interior, and the people are American nationals. The Governor and his staff are responsible for administration. A legislature of 15 elected chiefs (upper house) and 17 elected commoners (lower house) meets to pass limited legislation.

The people are of similar stock to the Western Samoans, have the *matai* system, and live in similar villages which, because of the mountainous nature of the land, tend to be more isolated than those in Western Samoa.

### Population

| 1900 | 5,700 |
| 1966 | 23,514 |

The climate and vegetation of Tutuila is similar to that of Western Samoa, with a rather higher rainfall (Pago-Pago 200″).

Land is held by families, and agriculture, practised on a subsistence basis, is the main source of livelihood. Of the 48,640 acres, 36,000 acres are cultivable. Much farming is done on land sloping by as much as 45°. The main crops are copra, taro, bananas, yam, breadfruit, and cocoa.

The most important sources of export income are canned tuna fish ($20 million in 1966), frozen fish, and fish meal. The plants at Pago-Pago employ several hundred Samoans. Fish is supplied to the canneries by Japanese, Korean, and Chinese catcher boats on contract.

Copra exports are small ($65,000 in 1966) and floor mats and handicrafts for sale to tourists provide a small income.

Few but regular shipping services call at Pago-Pago. There is a monthly steamer from New Zealand and Matson liners call every three weeks. Other cruise ships call.

The tourist industry is being encouraged and to foster this a 9,000-ft jet runway has been built at Tafuna. There is also a luxury hotel.

Education in Eastern Samoa is carried out largely by television.

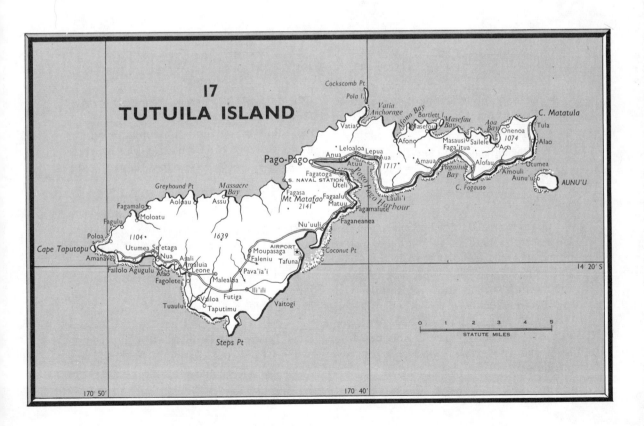

17
# TUTUILA ISLAND

# TONGA

**Size and Physical Nature:** Area 269 sq. miles, scattered over 20,000 sq. miles of ocean. About 150 islands, only 36 of which are inhabited.

The islands lie in two fairly parallel lines on top of two undersea ridges. The eastern chain consists of low coral islands and raised coral islands, e.g. Vava'u. The western chain is of high volcanic islands, e.g. Tofua (3,380 ft). Niuatoputapu, and Niuafo'ou are volcanic islands lying 200 miles north and north-west of Vava'u.

**Government:** Tonga is a self-governing kingdom. The present ruler is King Tupou IV. It is a British Protected State by virtue of a Treaty of Friendship ratified in 1901. The United Kingdom Government is represented by the British Consul. Major decisions are made by the King-in-Council, lesser ones by the Cabinet of six Ministers. Parliament consists of Cabinet Ministers, seven representatives of the nobles, and seven representatives of the people. Elections are held every three years.

There are three administrative divisions, Tongatapu, Ha'apai, and Vava'u, the last two having Tongan Governors. There are also local district and town officers.

**Population and Settlement:** The Tongan people are Polynesians and speak Tongan.

## Population

| Date | Tongans | Europeans | Others | Total |
|------|---------|-----------|--------|-------|
| 1840 | | | | 18,500 (Missionaries' estimate) |
| 1920 | | | | 23,128 |
| 1939 | | | | 34,130 (census) |
| 1956 | 55,156 | 277 | 1,405 | 56,838 (census) |
| 1964 | 71,000 | 200 | 800 | 72,000 (est.) |
| 1966 | | | | 77,585 (census) |

Annual rate of population increase 3.5 per cent. The inhabited islands except Eua are densely populated.

### Population (1966) and Density

| | | |
|---|---|---|
| Tongatapu | 48,485 | 484 per sq. mile |
| Ha'apai | 10,464 | 520 per sq. mile |
| Vava'u | 13,299 | 295 per sq. mile |
| Niuatoputapu | 1,389 | 230 per sq. mile |

Villages from 200 to 500 people are mostly on or near the sea shore, although they may be up to half a mile inland on the S.E. trade wind side of the islands. The houses are of varied construction, from oval-ended *fale* with thatched roofs and walls, to wooden or concrete walls and to European type with corrugated iron roofs. Water is obtained from wells and roof tanks. Most villages have piped water.

**Climate and Vegetation:** Annual average rainfall increases from 63″ at Tongatapu in the south to 101″ at Niuatoputapu in the north. Average annual temperature increases from 74°F at Tongatapu to 80°F at Niuatoputapu.

The S.E. trade winds blow for most of the year. There is a "dry season" from July to December, when droughts often occur.

Hurricanes occasionally affect the islands of the northern groups.

Much of Eua, Kao, Tofua and Late is forested. The other islands, where not planted, have secondary forest or bush fallow.

**Land Tenure and Farming:** All land belongs to the Crown and cannot be bought. Every male Tongan on reaching the age of 16 is

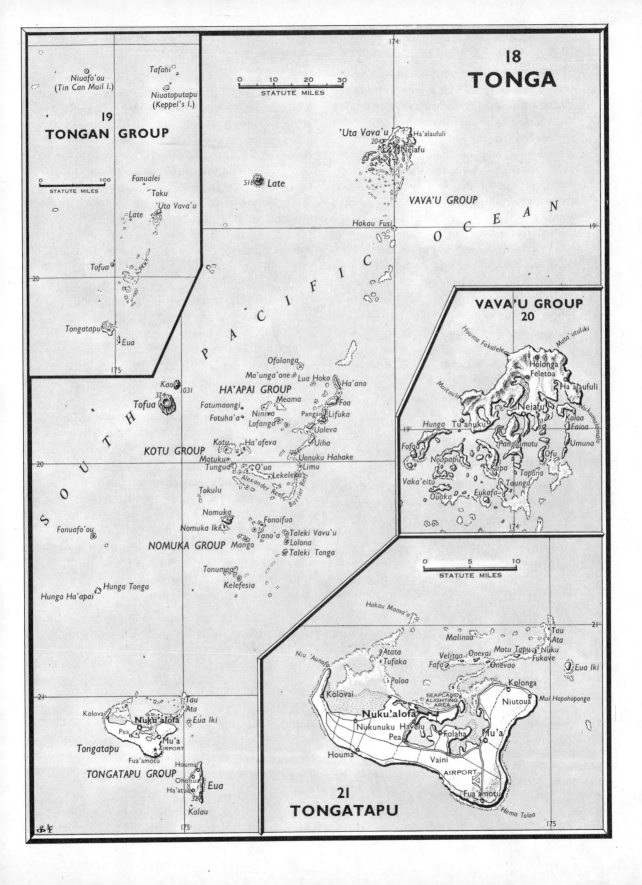

## 18
# TONGA

### 19
## TONGAN GROUP

Niuafo'ou
(Tin Can Mail I.)

Tafahi

Niuatoputapu
(Keppel's I.)

Fonualei
Toku
'Uta Vava'u
Late

Tofua

Tongatapu
Eua

STATUTE MILES
0   10   20   30

STATUTE MILES
0                100

'Uta Vava'u
204
Ha'alaufuli
Neiafu

518 Late

**VAVA'U GROUP**

Hakau Fusi

O  C  E  A  N

19

### VAVA'U GROUP
### 20

Houma Fakalele
Mata'utuliki
Holonga
Feletoa
Ha'alaufuli

Muitou'a
Neiafu
Nukumalolmalo

Hunga  Tu'anuku
Koloa
Faioa

19
Fofoa
Pangaimotu
Umuna

Noapapu
Ofu

Vaka'eitu
Kapa
Tapana
Taunga

Ouoka
Eukafa

174

SEAPCANE
ALIGHTING
AREA

S  O  U  T  H    P  A  C  I  F  I  C

Kao
1031
374 Tofua

Ofolanga
Mo'unga'one   Lua Hoko   Ha'ano
**HA'APAI GROUP**
Fatumaongi      Meama        Foa
Fotuha'a      Niniva        Lifuka
Lofanga    Pangai
Uoleva
Kotu   Ha'afeva    Uiha
**KOTU GROUP**
Matuku       Uonuku Hahake
Tungua    O'ua    Limu
Lekeleka
Tokulu    Alexander Reef      Barrier Reef
Nomuka
Nomuka Iki    Fonoifua
Tano'a   Taleki Vavu'u
**NOMUKA GROUP** Mango   Lolona
Taleki Tonga
Fonuafo'ou
Tonumea
Kelefesia
Hunga Tonga
Hunga Ha'apai

20

STATUTE MILES
0        5        10

Hakau Mama'o

21

Malinoa
Tau
Ata
Niu 'Aunofo
Atata    Velitoa  Onevai   Motu Tapu  Nuku
Tufaka              Onevao  Fukave
Fafa
Kolovai
Poloa
Kolonga
Nuku'alofa
Niutoua
Nukunuku Havelu
Mui Hopohoponga
Pea
Folaha   Mu'a
Houma
Vaini
AIRPORT
Fua'amotu
Homa Toloa

### 21
## TONGATAPU

Tau
Ata
Kolova
Eua Iki
**Nuku'alofa**
Pea
Mu'a
Tongatapu     AIRPORT
Fua'amotu
Houma
Ohonua    Eua
Ha'atua
Kalau

**TONGATAPU GROUP**

175

174

21

175

entitled to an allotment of eight and one quarter acres and a house site in a village. There are a small number of copra plantations leased by Europeans and churches.

Over 90 per cent of the people are concerned with farming, mainly on their own plots. Yams, taro, kumaras, manioc, bananas, breadfruit, pawpaw, kava, paper mulberry (for tapa cloth), and vegetables are grown in rotation. After two or three years a plot is allowed to revert to "bush fallow". Coconuts are widespread though not in the higher areas of Eua, Vava'u and the volcanic islands. About an eighth to a quarter of coconuts are used for food. The remainder is made into copra for export.

**Exports:**

|          | 1961          | 1963         |
|----------|---------------|--------------|
| Copra    | 17,411 tons   | 9,900 tons   |
| Bananas  | 179,652 cases | 92,930 cases |

Total Value (1963) £A958,876

**Industry:** There is no industry apart from the Government sawmill on Eua Island, a seasonal fruit pulp processing plant in Vava'u and a coconut dessicating and coir products plant.

**Towns:** The capital, Nuku'alofa (15,000), on Tongatapu, is the chief port and town and is the headquarters of trading firms, churches, and of government departments.

Neiafu (5,000), in Vava'u, has an excellent sheltered harbour.

**Communications:** Tonga is fairly isolated.

There is a fortnightly steamer service on the New Zealand, Fiji, Tonga, Niue, Samoa run and a monthly service by Government vessels between Tonga and Fiji. Copra ships and other ships call occasionally. Air services connect to Fiji and Samoa. Internally, inter-island communication is carried out by Government vessels and by cutters. A local radio station began operations in 1961. A tourist hotel has recently been built.

**Special Features:**

1. Niuafo'ou is "Tin Can Island" where, because of poor harbour facilities, a swimmer carried mail in a sealed "tin can" out to steamers. The island has had several volcanic eruptions and is now resettled after a period of 15 years.

2. Falcon Island, or "Jack in a Box" Island, an undersea volcano, appears above sea level from time to time.

3. Tongans in small whaleboats catch whales for the sale of meat during the whale migrations between July and October.

4. The islands are infested with the rhinoceros beetle, a serious pest of coconuts.

5. The Ha'amonga trilithon and large tombs at Mu'a are huge stone structures built in ancient times.

6. Tonga is one of the few countries associated with the British Commonwealth with a firmly established monarchy and in this respect is unique in the Pacific.

# TOKELAU ISLANDS

(excluding American Swains Island)
See Map Page 27

**Size and Physical Nature:** Area 4 sq. miles. Consists of three atolls, which encircle lagoons: Nukunono, 1,350 acres; Fakaofo, 650 acres; Atafu, 500 acres.

The reef islets on these atolls vary in length from 100 yards to four miles and are ten to 15 feet above sea level.

**Government:** The three atolls form a New Zealand dependency and the people are New

Zealand citizens. The Administrator is the New Zealand High Commissioner in Western Samoa. Local government is carried out on each atoll by an elected *Faipule* who is also magistrate. He is assisted by a village mayor, a village clerk, and other local officers.

**Population and Settlement:** The Tokelaus are a border area between Polynesia and Micronesia. The people are Polynesian and have some similarity with Samoans and an atoll culture similar to that of the Northern Cooks.

### Population

| Date | | | Total |
|------|------|-----|-------|
| 1956 | | | 1,618 |
| 1966 | Atafu | 616 | |
| | Fakaofo | 733 | |
| | Nukunono | 559 | 1,908 |

Only two Europeans, both missionaries, live in the group.

Density of Population 475 per sq. mile.

Settlement is confined to one islet on Nukunono and on Atafu. On Fakaofo, overcrowding has resulted in settling about 40 families on the neighbouring islet of Fenuafala. In all cases villages are near a reef passage which gives access to vessels and ocean fishing.

Houses are built of pandanus timber with walls and roofs of plaited pandanus leaves. The houses have gabled roofs similar to those in the Gilbert Islands. Water is provided from concrete rain tanks in the villages.

Government and mission schools provide education for almost 100 per cent of the children.

**Climate and Vegetation:**

| | |
|---|---|
| Average annual rainfall | 115″ |
| Highest annual rainfall | 177″ |
| Lowest annual rainfall | 87″ |
| Average temperature (January) | 82°F |
| Average temperature (July) | 82°F |

The islands lie in the zone of the S.E.

trades but from November to February north-east and northerly winds predominate.

Soils are almost entirely coral sand, with coconuts and pandanus the main vegetation.

**Land Tenure and Farming:** Land is held by the heads of families and may be sold to other families or to the Crown but not to foreigners. With the increase in population and the subdivision of families, land holdings become smaller.

There is no farming in the accepted sense. Atolls have little soil and apart from coconuts which grow out of the coral rock, the only food plants are a few breadfruit trees, pandanus, bananas and paw paws grown in man-made compost pits, supplemented by fish, fowls, and pigs, and imported flour and sugar.

**Exports:** Copra is the staple export.

| Date | Tons | Value |
|------|------|-------|
| 1961 | 155 | £2,981 |
| 1963–4 | 44 | £1,138 |
| 1966 | | £9,499 |

Postage stamps and plaited ware are a small source of income.

**Communications:** There is no regular shipping or air transport. Chartered ships call to trade and to transport officials. Occasional flying-boats visit the group for medical and other purposes. Local radio sets receive broadcasts from Western Samoa and each atoll has a radio station.

**Special Features:**
1. Fish and coconuts form almost entirely the diet of the people.
2. The Tokelauans were recently offered the choice of amalgamation with the Cook Islands or Western Samoa or complete independence, but chose to remain New Zealand citizens.
3. Due to overpopulation some Tokelauans are being resettled in New Zealand.

# COOK ISLANDS

**Size and Physical Nature:** Area 93 sq. miles. Fifteen islands scattered over about 850,000 sq. miles of ocean.

There are two distinct groups: the Northern Cooks consisting of seven atolls, six of which are inhabited; and the Southern Cooks, consisting of eight islands of which six are volcanic and two are atolls. Seven of these are inhabited.

The volcanic islands have a hilly interior and some fertile lowlands. They are surrounded by coral reefs and most have an elevated reef or *makatea* immediately behind the coastline.

### Area of Islands in Acres

| Northern Group | | Southern Group | |
|---|---|---|---|
| Penrhyn | 2,432 | Rarotonga | 16,602 |
| Manihiki | 1,344 | Mangaia | 12,800 |
| Pukapuka | 1,250 | Atiu | 6,654 |
| Rakahanga | 1,000 | Mitiaro | 5,500 |
| Palmerston | 500 | Mauke | 4,552 |
| Nassau | 300 | Aitutaki | 4,461 |
| Suwarrow | 100 | Manuae | 1,524 |
| | | Takutea | 302 |

**Government:** The Cook group became self-governing when the Cook Islands' Constitution was brought into force in August 1965. The people are New Zealand citizens and executive authority is vested in Her Majesty the Queen in right of New Zealand which is responsible for its external affairs and defence. A High Commissioner appointed by the Governor-General of New Zealand resides in Rarotonga.

Executive Government is carried out by a Cabinet consisting of a Premier and five other Ministers who are collectively responsible to the Legislative Assembly.

The Legislative Assembly consists of 22 members elected by universal suffrage from a common roll for both Maoris and Europeans and is presided over by a Speaker. Island Councils have been established on each of the main islands. A House of Arikis or chiefs was established in 1966.

**Population and Settlement:** The Maori people of the Cook Islands are Polynesians, closely related to the New Zealand Maori and have a similar tribal and chiefly system.

### Population

| Date | Maori | European |
|---|---|---|
| 1945 | 13,574 | 514 |
| 1956 | 16,373 | 307 (census) |
| 1963 | 18,890 | 324 (census) |
| 1966 | 19,251 | 320 (estimated) |

Density of Population 207 per sq. mile

| | | |
|---|---|---|
| Infant Mortality: | 1956 | 149 per 1,000 births |
| | 1963 | 50 per 1,000 births |
| Birth Rate: | 1963 | 47 per 1,000 |
| Death Rate: | 1963 | 8.75 per 1,000 |

Great progress has been made in recent years in reducing rates of infant mortality.

### Population of each island (1964)

| Northern Group | | Southern Group | |
|---|---|---|---|
| Penrhyn | 694 | Rarotonga | 9,733 |
| Manihiki | 1,089 | Mangaia | 2,097 |
| Pukapuka | 800 | Atiu | 1,404 |
| Rakahanga | 368 | Mitiaro | 331 |
| Palmerston | 102 | Mauke | 866 |
| Nassau | 113 | Aitutaki | 2,904 |
| Suwarrow | — | Manuae | 18 |
| | | Takutea | — |

The people live in villages which are mainly near the shore. Inland villages on Mauke and Atiu are exceptions. Housing varies through the group but the traditional type is rectangular, with walls of narrow branches of hibiscus tree and the roofs of thatched palm leaves. Other materials used are coral lime, timber, boxwood, and corrugated iron. Public buildings have iron roofs from which rain-water can be held in concrete tanks. Churches and schools are features of island life.

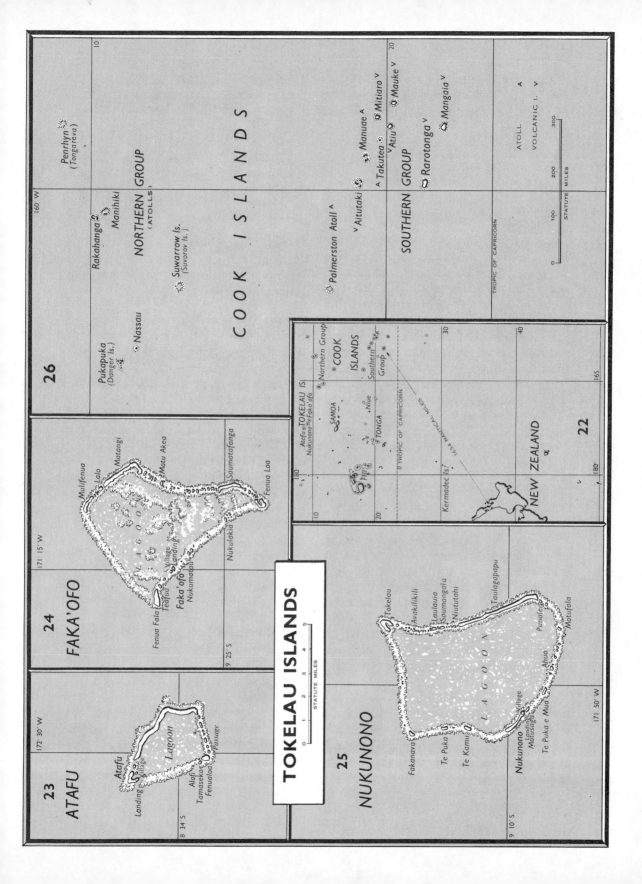

# TOKELAU ISLANDS

**23 ATAFU**

172 30' W
171 15' W

Matangi
Mulifenua
Lalo
Motu Akea

Atafu
Landing
Village
Lagoon
Tamasekoe
Alofi
Fenuafala Passage

8 34' S

0  1  2  3  4  5
STATUTE MILES

**24 FAKA'OFO**

Mulifenua
Matangi
Lalo
Motu Akea

L A G O O N

Fenua Fala
Teafua
Village
Landing
Fakaʻofo
Nukumatau

Saumatafanga
Fenua Loa
Nukulakia

9 25' S

**26**

160 W
10

Penrhyn
(Tongareva)

Rakahanga
Manihiki

**NORTHERN GROUP**
(ATOLLS)

Suwarrow Is.
(Suvorov Is.)

Pukapuka
(Danger Is.)
Nassau

C O O K   I S L A N D S

Palmerston Atoll ᴬ

ᵛ Aitutaki
Manuae ᴬ
ᴬ Takutea
ᵛ Atiu
Mitiaro ᵛ
ᵛ Mauke

Rarotonga ᵛ
Mangaia ᵛ

**SOUTHERN GROUP**

20

ATOLL        ᴬ
VOLCANIC I.  ᵛ

TROPIC OF CAPRICORN

0    100    200    300
STATUTE MILES

**22**

180
165

Atafu ⊛ TOKELAU IS.
Nukunono ⊛ Fakaʻofo
Northern Group
**COOK
ISLANDS**
Southern
Group
30

SAMOA
Niue
TONGA
Fiji
Kermadec Is.

TROPIC OF CAPRICORN

1463 NAUTICAL MILES

40

**NEW ZEALAND**

180

10
20

**25 NUKUNONO**

171 50' W

Tokelau
Avokilikili
Taulauia
Saumangalu
Niututahi

Fakanava
Te Puka
Te Kamu

Nukunono
Landing
Matusaga
Village
Te Puka e Mua
Ahua

L A G O O N

Pundes
Taulagapapu
Motufala

9 10' S

There are 23 village primary schools (roll 4,979 in 1964). Rarotonga has a secondary school and a teachers' college. All children attend school.

## Climate and Vegetation:

|  | Average Annual Rainfall | Average Temperature January | July |
|---|---|---|---|
| Pukapuka | 109″ | 82°F | 82°F |
| Rarotonga | 83″ | 78°F | 71°F |

The whole group lies in the zone of the S.E. trade winds. Rainfall varies considerably throughout the islands and the "hurricane" season from November to April is wetter than the rest of the year. From May to October the Southern Cooks have lower temperatures and humidities than the Northern Cooks. During the hurricane season tropical cyclones may affect the Southern group.

Vegetation in the Northern group is mainly coconuts, pandanus, and scrub. In the Southern islands few large timber trees remain and much of the land is covered with secondary forest, coconut palms, and food trees.

**Land Tenure and Farming:** Land, apart from that held by the Crown, is owned by native family groups. Sale of land is prohibited. Between 3,000 and 4,000 acres are leased to Maoris and Europeans. Farming and fishing are the main occupations. Although soils on the Southern islands are mainly fertile, some large areas cannot be used because they are steep or infertile areas on old raised coral reefs. For example, only one third of Rarotonga is farmable and only one half of Mangaia. The main food crops grown are swamp taro, kumaras, yams, manioc, and bananas.

Commercial crops for export are an important part of Cook Islands agriculture. Of these, citrus fruits are most important, followed by copra (mainly from the Northern atolls), tomatoes, and pineapples from Mangaia.

| Exports: | 1965 | |
|---|---|---|
| Citrus Fruits | 52,740 cases | £61,865 |
| Bananas | 6,031 cases | £7,734 |
| Pineapples | 8,834 cases | £9,043 |
| Tomatoes | 101,886 cases | £85,002 |
| Copra | 1,751 tons | £126,379 |
| Pearl Shell | 39 tons | £15,167 |
| Handicrafts | .. | £16,786 |
| Clothing | .. | £239,288 |
| Jewellery | .. | £1,756 |
| Fruit Juice | .. | £396,453 |

**Industry:** Two clothing factories and a fruit canning and juice factory are the most important industries. Two small firms manufacture shell jewellery.

**Towns:** Avarua on Rarotonga, with a population of 6,000 (1964) is the chief town and administrative centre. It is the main port of call, though only an open roadstead. At Avarua is the central cool store for perishable fruit exports and the Rarotonga Hotel.

**Communications:** Lack of adequate communications and poor harbours are the main problems in the Cook Islands. The New Zealand Government vessel *Moana Roa* calls regularly about once a month. Matson liners call regularly and cargo ships occasionally. Small inter-island vessels serve the outer islands.

There are airstrips on Aitutaki and Rarotonga. Rarotonga has a radio station which communicates with other sub-stations on the other islands.

**Special Features:**
1. Nearly 8,000 Cook Islanders now live in New Zealand.
2. Although the Cook Islands are administered as a single entity each island has distinct characteristics and dialect. The Rarotongan language is used as the standard dialect, but the language of the Pukapuka is very different.
3. Motor cycles and scooters are widely used.

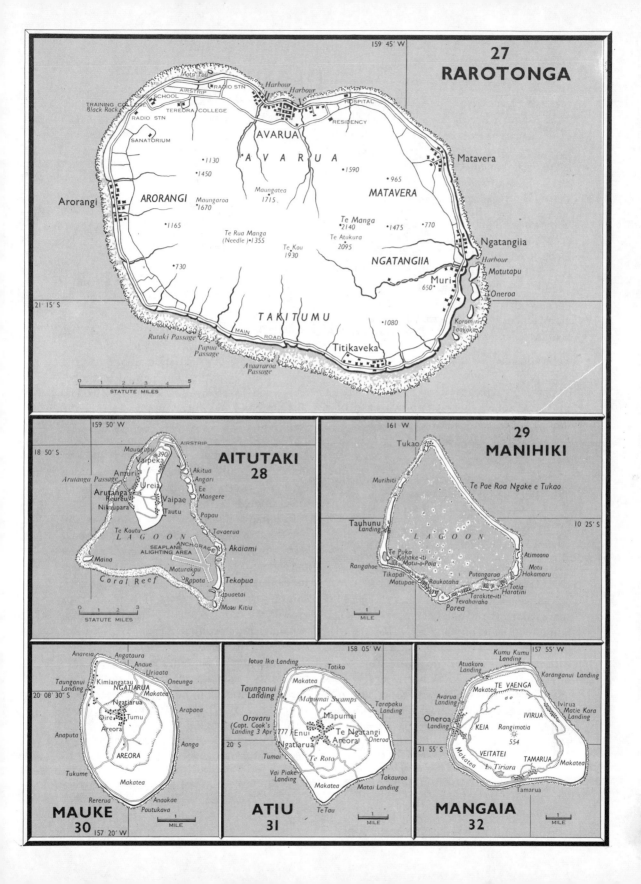

## 27
## RAROTONGA

159° 45' W

Mota Tou
AIRSTRIP
RADIO STN
Harbour Harbour
TRAINING COLLEGE
INSIDE SCHOOL
Black Rock
TEREORA COLLEGE
HOSPITAL
RESIDENCY
RADIO STN
SANATORIUM

AVARUA

A V A R U A

•1130
•1450
•1590
•965
Matavera

Arorangi

ARORANGI

Maungaroa
•1670
Maungatea
1715

MATAVERA

Te Manga
•2140
•1475
•770

•1165

Te Rua Manga
(Needle )•1355
Te Atukura
2095

Ngatangiia

Te Kou
1930

NGATANGIIA

Harbour
Motutapu

•730

Muri
650•
Oneroa

21° 15' S

T A K I T U M U

•1080

Koromiri
Taakoka

MAIN ROAD
Rutaki Passage
Papua Passage
Titikaveka

Avaavaroa Passage

0   1   2   3   4   5
STATUTE MILES

---

159° 50' W

18° 50' S

Maungapu
AIRSTRIP
•390
Vaipeka
Amuri
Akitua
Arutanga Passage
Ureia
Angari
Ee
Arutanga
Reureu
Mangere
Nikaupara
Vaipae
Tautu
Papau

## AITUTAKI
## 28

Te Koutu

Tavaerua

L A G O O N

ANCHORAGE
SEAPLANE
ALIGHTING AREA
Akaiami

Maina

Moturakau
Rapota

Tekopua

C o r a l   R e e f

Tapuaetai

Motu Kitiu

0   1   2   3
STATUTE MILES

---

161° W

Tukao

## 29
## MANIHIKI

Murihiti

Te Pae Roa Ngake e Tukao

10° 25' S

Tauhunu
Landing

L A G O O N

Te Puka
Kohake-iti
Motu-o-Paia
Atimoono

Rangahoe
Motu
Hakamaru

Tikapa
Matupae
Putangaroa

Raukotaha

Totia
Haratini

Tarakite-iti
Tevahavaha
Porea

1
MILE

---

Anareia
Angataura
Anaue
Uriaata

Taunganui
Landing
Kimiangatau
NGATIARUA
Makatea
Oneunga

Anaue
Oire
Ngatiarua
Tumu
Arapaea

Anaputa
Areora

Aanga

AREORA

Tukume

Rererua
Anaokae
Poutukava
Makatea

## MAUKE
## 30
157° 20' W

20° 08' 30" S

---

158° 05' W

Iotua Ika Landing
Totiko

Taunganui
Landing
Makatea

Mapumai Swamps
Tarapaku
Landing

Orovaru
(Capt. Cook's
Landing 3 Apr
Mapumai

Te Ngatangi
Areora
Oneroa

Enui
Ngatiarua
777

Tumai
Te Roto

Vai Piake
Landing
Takauroa
Matai Landing
Makatea

Te Tau

20° S

## ATIU
## 31

1
MILE

---

157° 55' W

Kumu Kumu
Landing
Atuakoro
Landing
Korarganui Landing

Avarua
Landing
Makatea
TE VAENGA

Ivirua
Matie Kora
Landing

Oneroa
Landing

KEIA
IVIRUA

Rangimotia
554

Makatea

VEITATEI
L. Tiriara

TAMARUA
Makatea

21° 55' S

Tamarua

## MANGAIA
## 32

1
MILE

# NIUE ISLAND

**Size and Physical Nature:** Area 100 sq. miles. Niue is a raised coral island, perched on top of a submerged volcano and surrounded by very deep water. A fringing reef encircles the island and behind this 70-ft cliffs rise to a terrace. A sharp slope then rises to a saucer-shaped central plateau about 200 ft high.

**Government:** Niue is a New Zealand dependency administered by the New Zealand Department of Island Territories through a Resident Commissioner at Alofi. An elected Island Assembly has control over all finance. An executive committee is responsible for the main functions of government. Like Cook Islanders, Niueans are New Zealand citizens.

**Population and Settlement:** Niueans are Polynesians of a shorter built, wirier type than Tongans or Samoans. They have no rank or title system save that of *Patu*, or head of a family, which every married man holds.

### Population

| | |
|---|---|
| 1900 | 4,200 |
| 1928 | 3,747 |
| 1949 (census) | 4,634 (45 Europeans) |
| 1956 (census) | 4,650 (57 Europeans) |
| 1966 (census) | 5,194 (95 Europeans) |

| | |
|---|---|
| Density of Population | 51 per sq. mile |
| Infant Mortality: 1945 | 119 per 1,000 births |
| 1963 | 18 per 1,000 births |
| Birth Rate: 1963 | 43 per 1,000 |
| Death Rate: 1963 | 6.3 per 1,000 |

The people live in 13 villages in clearings spaced along the 40 miles of coastal road. The houses had walls of white *puga* (missionaries taught the use of this burnt coral limestone), with roofs of thatch or corrugated iron. Most houses were destroyed by hurricanes in 1959 and 1960 and new houses with concrete floors, walls of concrete, concrete blocks, fibrolite, or timber and fibrolite roofs, have been built. Each new house has a 400-gallon rainwater tank.

A church is the focus of each village. There are seven village primary schools (roll 1,389 in 1966), and a high school and teachers' training college at Alofi.

**Climate and Vegetation:**

| | |
|---|---|
| Average annual rainfall | 79″ |
| Highest annual rainfall | 133″ |
| Lowest annual rainfall | 32″ |
| Average temperature (January) | 81°F |
| Average temperature (July) | 76°F |

The island lies in the zone of the S.E. trades with an April-November dry season during which droughts often occur. It is occasionally visited by hurricanes during the summer months, most recently in 1959 and 1960.

About 8,000 acres of the islands are covered with heavy forest, including excellent timber trees such as ebony and other hardwoods. Their roots grow down into fissures in the coral rock.

**Land Tenure and Farming:** Land is held by individual families and may not be purchased by non-Niueans. Holdings are often split up and scattered.

Farming is hindered by the scarcity of soil and the shortage of water. Around the coastal terrace only small pockets of soil occur among the exposed coral. Even on the central plateau the soil is thin and porous with coral rock showing through in places. The main crops grown are taro, kumaras, manioc, yams, bananas, and coconuts. Yields are often low because of drought.

A large area of land on the central plateau, previously overcropped and exhausted, has been brought back to use by the Government with the aid of disc ploughing, legumes, fertilisers, and shade trees.

A Development Board is promoting agricultural improvement.

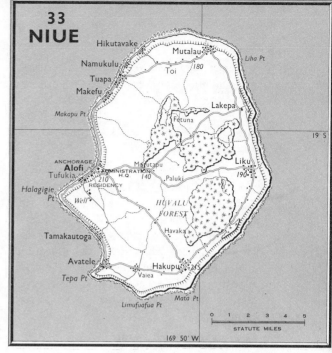

### Approximate Land Use
Forest – 8,000 acres
Suitable for Agriculture – 48,000 acres
(possibly ⅕th ploughable)
Not suitable for Agriculture – 8,000 acres.

| Exports: | **1956** | | **1965** | |
|---|---|---|---|---|
| | *Tons* | *Value* | *Tons* | *Value* |
| Copra | 831 | £49,000 | 347 | £23,000* |
| Plaited Ware | | | | |
| (Baskets, hats, | | | | |
| mats) | | £6,321 | | £7,400 |
| Bananas | | £4,070 | | £6,400 |
| Kumara | | | | |
| (varies widely) | | £260 | | £6,700 |
| Taro, Yam | | | | £1,415 |

*Copra exports recommenced during 1962, after a complete cessation following damage to coconuts in hurricanes of 1959 and 1960.

**Industry:** Home weaving of baskets, mats and hats, and sawmilling by the administration are the only industries.

**Towns:** Alofi, the centre of administration, is a village of 1,200 people. The government offices, schools, hospital, stores, post office, church, and wharf sheds are the main buildings.

**Communications:** There is no harbour or airfield. Ships lie off the reef if the sea is calm and passengers and goods are lightered ashore. A monthly steamer service from New Zealand via Fiji, Tonga, and Samoa is the only shipping, apart from occasional visits by mission boats and the New Zealand Government vessel. Villages are linked by telephone. A radio station is being established.

**Special Features:**
1. About 200 to 300 Niueans of whom over half are males, emigrate to New Zealand every year. This number almost equals the natural population increase in Niue.
2. Recent research has shown that Niue has a very high level of natural radioactivity. The level is much higher than in other areas and has been so for many years.

# FRENCH POLYNESIA

**Size and Physical Nature:** Area 1,520 sq. miles. 130 islands scattered over 1,544,400 sq. miles of ocean. Comprises:

*The Society Islands:* Windward Group (six islands), of which Tahiti (386 sq. miles) and Moorea (51 sq. miles) are the largest.
Leeward Group (nine islands), of which Raiatea (93 sq. miles) and Bora Bora (14.5 sq. miles) are the largest.

*The Marquesas:* Nine islands. Hiva-oa (93 sq. miles).
*The Tuamoto Archipelago* (305 sq. miles): About 80 atolls.
*The Gambier Group* (11.5 sq. miles): Five islands.
*The Austral Islands:* Five islands. Tubuai (18 sq. miles), Rapa (8.5 sq. miles).

Apart from the coral atolls of the Tuamotus the islands are mainly mountainous and of volcanic origin with, except the Marquesas, surrounding coral reefs. Very rugged and dissected, the islands rise to 4,265 ft (Mt Keaui) in the Marquesas, and 7,338 ft (Mt Orohena) on Tahiti. The larger islands have a number of short rivers.

**Government:** French Polynesia is an overseas territory of France. The people are French nationals and have representation in the French parliament. There is a local elected Assembly of 30 members, and a Council of Government, chaired by the Governor, consisting of five members elected by the Assembly. The five administrative areas are divided into districts which have elected councils.

**Population and Settlement:**
### Population

| | | |
|---|---|---|
| 1926 | | 37,300 |
| 1946 | | 55,734 |
| 1956 | | 73,201 |
| 1962 Windward Islands | 52,068 | |
| Leeward Islands | 16,177 | |
| Marquesas Islands | 4,837 | |
| Tuamotu-Gambier Islands | 6,609 | |
| Austral Islands | 4,371 | |
| Total | | 84,062 |

The native people are Polynesians and make up 85 per cent of the total. Asians, mainly Chinese, make up 7 per cent. Europeans and others 8 per cent.

Tahiti with over half the total population is the most important island. Population density 56 per sq. mile; on Tahiti 120 per sq. mile.

The people are village dwellers, and the villages are mainly near the coast.

**Climate and Vegetation:**

| | | |
|---|---|---|
| Average annual rainfall | Papeete | 64.1″ |
| Average temperature | Papeete (January) | 80°F |
| | (July) | 77°F |

The islands lie in the zone of the S.E. trades, which, while moderating the temperature, bring higher rainfall to the windward sides of the islands.

Apart from the coconut- and pandanus-covered atolls the high islands are forested, with areas of dry grassland. Steep, jagged mountains of bare rock are common.

**Land Tenure and Farming:** The native people own 85 per cent of the land and have a land holding system under which 70 per cent is owned on a communal basis. Much of the land is steep but coastal plains and valleys are suitable for agriculture.

Village agriculture is of a subsistence nature based on root crops, fruit, and coconut. Commercial crops are of growing importance. In the Tuamotus copra is the only commercial export (apart from pearl shell), but on the high islands vanilla and coffee (Arabica) are also important.

Vanilla grows well in the valleys, particularly in the Windward islands. Coffee is grown chiefly in Tahiti, Moorea, and in the Austral islands.

Livestock is limited because of the small areas of pasture. There are about 10,000 cattle and a similar number of pigs. Several dairy farms supply milk to Papeete.

**Exports:**         **1962**

| | |
|---|---|
| Phosphate | 326,735 tons |
| Copra | 26,855 tons |
| Pearl Shell | 298 tons |
| Vanilla | 180 tons |

The total value of these exports was 971,549,000 francs.

Tourist revenue brought in an additional 401,000,000 francs.

**Industry:** The leading industry is phosphate mining on the island of Makatea in the Tuamoto group. Here phosphate is mined and loaded in much the same way as in Nauru Island and Ocean Island.

Other industries include plants for making coconut oil, soap, grated coconut, beer, and aerated drinks. Handicrafts and service industries connected with the tourist trade are expanding rapidly.

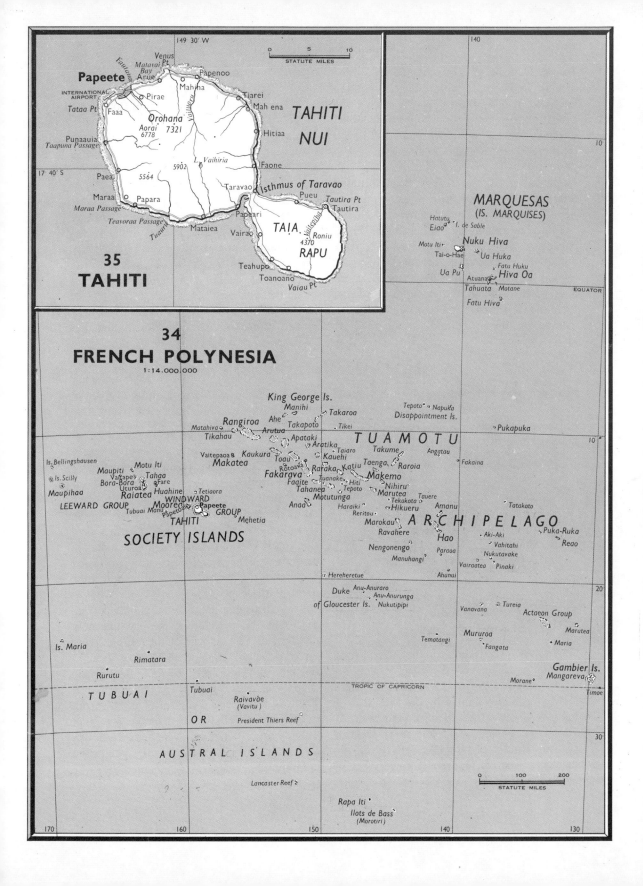

## 35 TAHITI

149 30' W

Venus Pt
Papeete
Matavai Bay
Arue
INTERNATIONAL AIRPORT
Tataa Pt
Faaa
Pirae
Mahina
Papenoo
Tiarei
Mah ena
Hitiaa

Orohana 7321
Aorai 6778

TAHITI NUI

L. Vaihiria
5902
5564

17 40' S
Paea
Papara
Maraa
Maraa Passage
Mataiea
Teavoraa Passage
Tuauru
Papeari
Vairao
Taravao
Isthmus of Taravao
Pueu
Tautira Pt
Tautira

TAIA
Roniu 4370

RAPU

Teahupo
Toanoano
Vaiau Pt

STATUTE MILES
0 5 10

Punaauia
Taapuna Passage

## 34 FRENCH POLYNESIA
### 1:14,000,000

MARQUESAS
(IS. MARQUISES)

Hatutu
Eiao
I. de Sable
Motu Iti
Nuku Hiva
Tai-o-Hae
Ua Huka
Ua Pu
Fatu Huku
Hiva Oa
Atuana
Tahuata
Motane
EQUATOR
Fatu Hiva

King George Is.
Manihi
Ahe
Takaroa
Takapoto
Tepoto
NapuKa
Disappointment Is.
Rangiroa
Matahiva
Arutua
Tikahau
Tikei
Pukapuka
Apataki
Aratika
Vaitepaoa
Kaukura
Toau
Kauehi
Taiaro
Takume
Angatau
Makatea
Rotoava
Katiu
Taenga
Raroia
Fakaina
Fakarava
Rafaka
Tuanake
Hiti
Makemo
Faaite
Tahanea
Tepoto
Nihiru
Marutea
Tauere
Anaa
Motutunga
Haraiki
Tekokota
Amanu
Tatakoto
Reritou
Hikueru
Marokau
Puka-Ruka
Ravahere
Hao
Aki-Aki
Reao
Vahitahi
Nengonengo
Paraoa
Nukutavake
Manuhangi
Vairaatea
Pinaki
Hereheretue
Ahunui

WINDWARD
Papeete
GROUP
TAHITI
Mehetia

Is. Bellingshausen
Is. Scilly
Maupiti
Motu Iti
Vahapes
Tahaa
Bora-Bora
Fare
Uturoa
Maupihaa
Raiatea
Huahine
Tetiaora
Moorea
LEEWARD GROUP
Tubuai Manu
Papeto

SOCIETY ISLANDS

TUAMOTU

ARCHIPELAGO

Duke
Anu-Anuraro
of Gloucester Is.
Anu-Anurunga
Nukutipipi
Vanavana
Tureia
Actaeon Group
Marutea
Tematangi
Mururoa
Maria
Fangata

Gambier Is.
Mangareva
Morane
Timoe

TROPIC OF CAPRICORN

Is. Maria
Rimatara
Rurutu

TUBUAI
Tubuai
Raivavae
(Vavitu)
President Thiers Reef

OR

AUSTRAL ISLANDS

Lancaster Reef

STATUTE MILES
0 100 200

Rapa Iti
Ilots de Bass
(Morotiri)

**Towns:** Papeete (25,000) on Tahiti is the capital and main port. Its population fluctuates widely due to leave visits by the French Army and Navy.      Other chief settlements are Uturoa (Raiatea I.), Taiohae (Nuku Hiva I.), Mataura (Tubuai I.).

**Communications:** Several overseas shipping lines call at Papeete. Inter-island communications are maintained by schooners.

Tahiti has an international airport at Faoa, constructed on a filled-in lagoon and capable of handling modern jet airliners. There are regular services with France, New Zealand, Samoa, the United States, and Australia. Inter-island services are flown by seaplane. The aerodrome at Uturoa can be used by DC-4's.

**Special Features:**

1. Captain James Cook observed the transit of the planet Venus at Point Venus on Tahiti in 1768.
2. Thor Heyerdahl's raft *Kon Tiki* was wrecked on Raroia Island in the Tuamotus after drifting from Peru.
3. The islands are rich in ancient stone platforms, monuments, and carvings.
4. The Marquesas, probably more than any other group in the Pacific, suffered depopulation at the end of the 18th century and the beginning of the 19th, due to the effects of alcohol and disease introduced by the whalers.
5. France has established a nuclear test base at Mururoa in the Tuamotus, and has tested several bombs.

# HAWAIIAN ISLANDS

**Size and Physical Nature:** Area 6,415 sq. miles. Eight inhabited islands and a number of rocky islets make up the archipelago. The main islands are:

| | |
|---|---|
| Hawaii | 4,030 sq. miles |
| Maui | 728 sq. miles |
| Oahu | 604 sq. miles |
| Kauai | 555 sq. miles |
| Molokai | 260 sq. miles |
| Lanai | 141 sq. miles |
| Niihau | 72 sq. miles |
| Kahoolawe | 45 sq. miles |

These islands are volcanic and mountainous or hilly, rising to 13,784 ft on Hawaii Island. They are partly encircled by coral reefs and have several active volcanoes.

**Government:** The islands are the 50th state of the United States of America, having an elected delegate to the U.S. Congress. There is a Governor appointed by the President of the U.S.A. Local legislation is in the hands of an elected Senate of 25 members and an elected House of Representatives of 51 members. The islands were a kingdom until

1893 and were annexed by the U.S.A. in 1898, attaining statehood in 1959.

**Population and Settlement:** The people, all of whom are American citizens, are very mixed racially, most being descendants of early European settlers, whalers, and of Asian people originally brought in to work on sugar and pineapple plantations. Native Hawaiians (Polynesians; 10,000) form a very small part of the population and are slowly decreasing. The Asians are now in varied occupations, a few are very wealthy and some are in Parliament.

Overall population density is 120 per sq. mile, but the population is very unevenly distributed, 82 per cent of the people living on tiny Oahu Island, three-fifths of these in the city of Honolulu. Hawaii, the largest island, has only eight per cent of the people. There is a marked movement of people from rural areas to cities. There is a very high literacy rate (98 per cent). Settlements are in the form of dispersed farms, plantation communities, villages, towns, and cities.

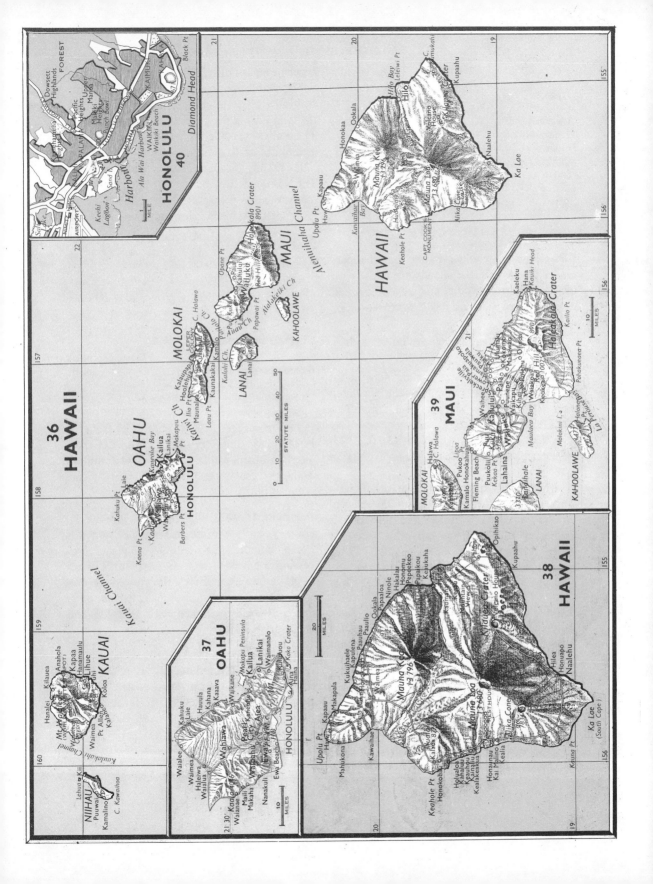

### Population

|                              | 1950    | 1964    | 1966    |
|------------------------------|---------|---------|---------|
| Japanese                     | 184,611 | 207,950 |         |
| Caucasian                    | 114,793 | 260,953 |         |
| Hawaiian and part-Hawaiian   | 86,091  | 110,930 |         |
| Filipino                     | 61,071  | 72,437  |         |
| Chinese                      | 32,376  | 40,016  |         |
| Others                       | 20,852  | 21,806  |         |
| Total                        | 499,794 | 714,092 | 756,000 |

Birth Rate 26 per 1,000
Death Rate 5.5 per 1,000
Rate of Increase 2.4%

**Climate and Vegetation:** Lying near the margin of the tropics, the islands are in the path of the N.E. trade winds and have a marked wet windward side and dry leeward side. For example:

| Average annual rainfall windward Oahu | 83″ |
|---|---|
| Average annual rainfall leeward Oahu | 20″ |

Irrigation is necessary for farming in the dry areas, the water being brought by tunnels from the wet side. Temperatures range from 56°F to 88°F.

Rainfall increases with altitude (e.g. Mt Waialeale on Kauai Island, has an average of 440″ per year).

Windward slopes and flats, where not cultivated, are forested. About 25 per cent of the country is forested and this area is protected for water conservation and for natural beauty. The leeward sides of the islands, where not cultivated, are in grassland and scrub.

**Land Tenure and Farming:** In 1846 King Kamehameha III divided all land between himself and his chiefs. He further divided his into "Crown" (for his use) and "Government" (which could be sold). Europeans bought most of the rich land during the last century or married into landowning chiefly families.

Land is very expensive and can be bought both privately and from the state. Most buildings in Honolulu are on leasehold land.

Only a third of the land is farmed. Less than 10 per cent is cultivated, for sugar and pineapple plantations, market vegetables, rice, tropical fruits, and coffee. Thirty per cent of the land is used for grazing the 260,000 cattle. There are some 20 commercial grazing ranches and about 80 commercial dairy farms, the latter mainly on Oahu, supplying town milk. The value of livestock products is only one tenth of the total farm income, which is dominated by pineapples and sugar.

### Cropland Products

| Sugar       | 73 per cent |
|-------------|-------------|
| Pineapples  | 22 per cent |
| Other crops | 5 per cent  |

Most of the coffee is grown at Kona on Hawaii Island.

**Exports and Tourism (1965):**

| Sugar | 175 million dollars |
|---|---|
| Pineapples (canned and juice) | 119 million dollars |
| Coffee, Fruits, Flowers, Garments, Hides and Skins, Wallboard, Fish, etc. | 47 million dollars |

Imports exceed exports but money from the huge tourist industry (260 million dollars a year) and from military spending (460 million dollars a year) more than balances the accounts (1965).

**Industry:** Hawaii is a thriving commercial country and, though having no minerals except bauxite, has manufacturing and processing industries, such as sugar mills, pineapple canneries, and factories concerned with foodstuffs, fertilisers, chemicals, fish canning, and activities concerned with shipping and the tourist industry.

**Towns:** Honolulu (343,000) on Oahu, is a rapidly growing modern city. It is the commercial, tourist, and university centre. Waikiki Beach is world famous. Pearl Harbour is its fine port and a U.S. Naval Base. Hilo (25,000) on the island of Hawaii is the second largest centre.

**Communications:** Hawaii is a crossroads of

the Pacific and is well served by shipping lines and transpacific air services. Daily sea and air services link the islands themselves.

**Special Features:**

1. Hawaii has some of the world's largest volcanoes. Mauna Loa and Kilauea on Hawaii Island are active. Kilauea has a lake of molten lava. Haleakala on Maui Island is dormant but its huge crater rift, five miles across and 3,000 ft deep, is the largest in the world. These volcanoes are in the Hawaii National Park.

2. The University of Hawaii including the East-West Centre had 17,000 students in 1965.

3. 600,000 tourists in 1965 are expected to reach 1 million by 1970.

4. Hawaii is the most highly commercialised island group in the Pacific.

5. Hawaii has a large surplus of unattached males. Single males 14 years of age or more outnumber single females by 91 per cent.

6. Members of the Armed Forces and dependants comprise 120,000 of the population.

# FIJI ISLANDS

**Size and Physical Nature:** Area 7,055 sq. miles (includes Rotuma, a dependency). Some 320 islands, only about 100 of which are inhabited. The islands can be divided into:

|  | sq. miles |
|---|---|
| Viti Levu and numerous small islands | 4,053 |
| Vanua Levu | 2,137 |
| Taveuni and small islands | 168 |
| Lomaivitu Group (about 12 islands in the Koro Sea, including Ovalau) | 158 |
| Kandavu | 157 |
| Ono | 12 |
| Lau Group (57 islands) | 178 |
| Yasawas (20 islands) | |

The islands are mainly mountainous (Mt Victoria, 4,341 ft), formed from volcanic and sedimentary materials deposited on a submarine platform.

Atolls and coral islands occur in the Lau Group and coral reefs encircle most of the islands. Viti Levu and Vanua Levu have several large rivers, alluvial valleys and deltas, e.g. Rewa, Sigatoka.

**Government:** Fiji is a British Crown Colony. It has a Governor who is assisted by an Executive and a Council of Ministers which makes laws. This council consists of the Governor, not more than 4 representatives of the Government, and 36 representatives of the people (10 Europeans, 14 Fijians, and 12 Indians, 34 of whom are elected by the people, and 2 of whom are elected by the Council of Chiefs). The colony is divided into four divisions (Northern, Eastern, Western, and Southern) for administration, each under a divisional Commissioner and District Officers.

In addition the Fijians have 14 provincial chiefs, and district chiefs. Also village headmen selected by village council. The Great Council of Chiefs meets every two years. One task is to nominate seven to ten Fijians for the Governor to select five for the Legislative Council.

**Population and Settlement:** The native Fijian people are Melanesian although those of the Lau group are strongly Polynesian.

### Total Population (Census)

|  | 1956 | 1966 |
|---|---|---|
| Indians | 169,403 | 240,960 |
| Fijians | 148,134 | 202,176 |
| Europeans | 6,402 | 6,590 |
| Mixed | 7,810 | 9,687 |
| Other Islanders | 5,320 | 6,095 |
| Rotumans | 4,422 | 5,797 |
| Chinese | 4,155 | 5,149 |
| Others | 91 | 273 |
| Total | 345,737 | 476,727 |

Rate of Increase 3.6%
Birth Rate 36 per 1,000
Death Rate 6 per 1,000

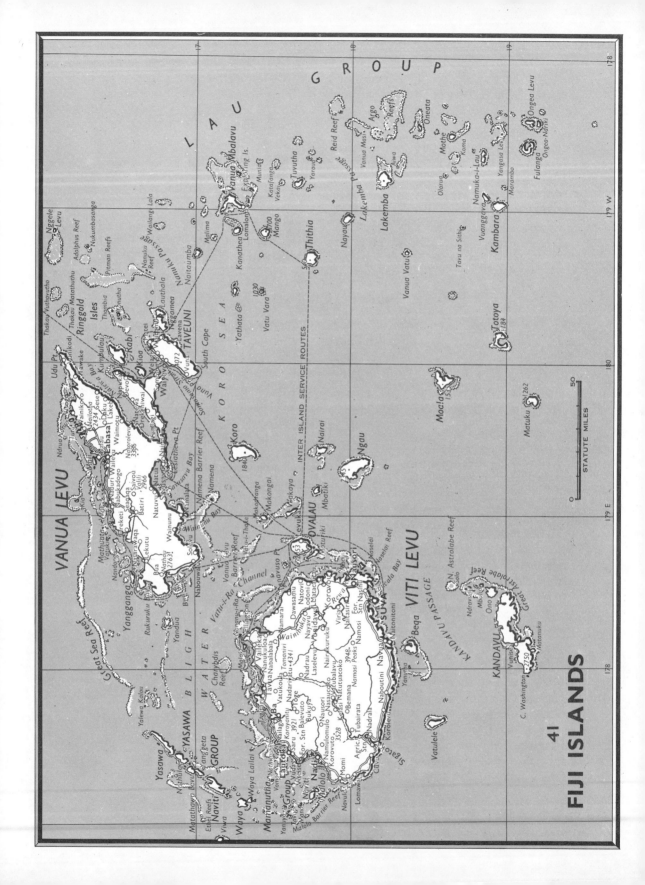

# FIJI ISLANDS

41

L A U   G R O U P

VANUA LEVU

VITI LEVU

KANDAVU

YASAWA GROUP

Mamanutha Group

Navit Group

KORO SEA

BLIGH   WATER

KANDAVU PASSAGE

STATUTE MILES

INTER ISLAND SERVICE ROUTES

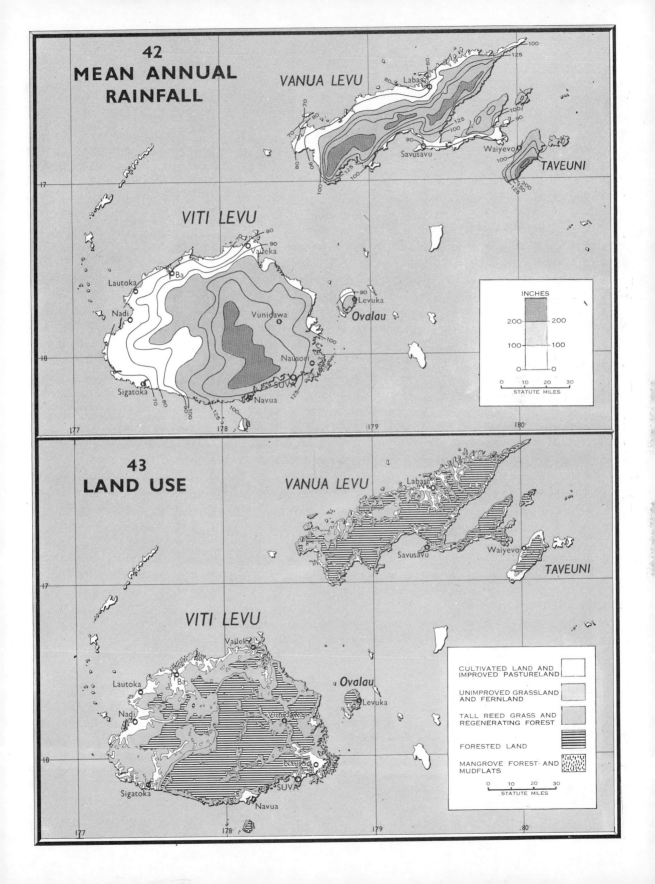

## 42
## MEAN ANNUAL RAINFALL

VANUA LEVU

Labasa

Savusavu

Waiyevo

TAVEUNI

17

VITI LEVU

Vaileka

Ba

Lautoka

Levuka

Nadi

Ovalau

Vuniqawa

Nausori

SUVA

18

Sigatoka

Navua

INCHES

200        200

100        100

0          0

0   10  20  30
STATUTE MILES

177        178        179        180

## 43
## LAND USE

VANUA LEVU

Labasa

Savusavu

Waiyevo

TAVEUNI

17

VITI LEVU

Vaileka

Ovalau

Lautoka

Ba

Levuka

Nadi

Vuniqawa

18

Nausori

Sigatoka

SUVA

Navua

CULTIVATED LAND AND
IMPROVED PASTURELAND

UNIMPROVED GRASSLAND
AND FERNLAND

TALL REED GRASS AND
REGENERATING FOREST

FORESTED LAND

MANGROVE FOREST AND
MUDFLATS

0   10  20  30
STATUTE MILES

177        178        179        180

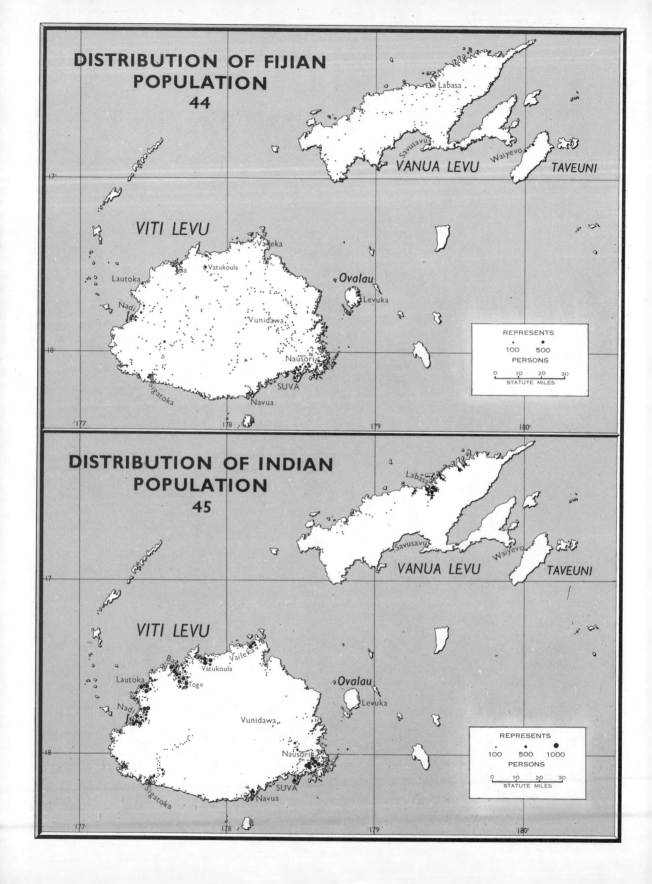

DISTRIBUTION OF FIJIAN
POPULATION
44

VITI LEVU

VANUA LEVU

TAVEUNI

Labasa

Savusavu

Waiyevo

Vaileka

Ba Vatukoula

Lautoka

Nadi

Ovalau

Levuka

Vunidawa

Nausori

Sigatoka

SUVA

Navua

REPRESENTS
•         ●
100     500
PERSONS

0    10    20    30
STATUTE MILES

DISTRIBUTION OF INDIAN
POPULATION
45

VITI LEVU

VANUA LEVU

TAVEUNI

Labasa

Savusavu

Waiyevo

Vaileka

Ba Vatukoula

Lautoka    Toge

Nadi

Ovalau

Levuka

Vunidawa

Nausori

Sigatoka

SUVA

Navua

REPRESENTS
•       ●       ⬤
100    500    1000
PERSONS

0    10    20    30
STATUTE MILES

The dominant racial group is Indian. Indians were brought to Fiji between 1879 and 1916 as indentured labourers to work on cotton and sugar plantations. Many chose to stay and they now play the main role in sugar production and in transport and commerce.

### Population of Indians and Fijians

| Date | Indians | Fijians |
|------|---------|---------|
| 1901 | 17,105 | 94,937 |
| 1921 | 60,634 | 84,475 |
| 1944 | 113,147 | 113,179 |
| 1964 | 228,176 | 189,169 |
| 1965 | 235,338 | 194,998 |

Overall population density 67 per sq. mile but settlement is concentrated round the coast, on alluvial flats, and up river valleys.

The Fijians live in coastal and riverbank villages of from 20 to 600 people. Houses are of thatch built on a raised earth foundation.

The Indians live in dispersed farmhouses on the alluvial flats and foothills, mainly in the dry western areas of Viti Levu and Vanua Levu, and in the sugarmill towns. All races live in Suva.

There is an extensive system of primary and secondary schools and of teacher training. A university opens in 1968.

**Climate and Vegetation:** Lying in the S.E. trade wind area, the larger and more mountainous islands have marked "wet" and "dry" sides. The winds drop their moisture on the windward side. There are three distinct climatic zones:

(a) "Wet zone", on the windward side. Rainfall is high and seasonal variation small. Humidity is high and daily temperature range small.

(b) "Dry zone", on the leeward side. Rainfall is lower with marked seasonal variation. Humidity is lower and daily range of temperature greater.

(c) The "small low islands". Rainfall is similar to that of the "dry zone" but seasonal variation is less. The daily range of temperature is similar to the "wet zone".

In January, February, and March the Equatorial front often brings north-westerly winds and occasional hurricanes occur.

| | Suva (wet zone) | Lautoka (dry zone) | Makogai (small island) |
|---|---|---|---|
| Average annual rainfall | 123″ | 70″ | 78″ |
| Average temperature (January) | 80°F | 81°F | 81°F |
| Average temperature (July) | 74°F | 75°F | 76°F |

Highest daily rainfall 36.5″ at Navai near Mt Victoria (1938)

Natural vegetation is related to the rainfall. The south-eastern and central parts of Viti Levu and Taveuni and the central and southern part of Vanua Levu, except the coastal areas, are covered in tropical rain forest. The remainder is tropical grassland of various kinds, coconuts or crops, with coastal areas of mangroves. The smaller islands are in forest and coconuts.

**Land Tenure and Farming:** Fijians have a tribal or clan system with a chief at its head. Each village consists of a clan or group of clans. Most land in Fiji is owned by these clan units. In 1874 the Fijian chiefs ceded Fiji to Britain on condition that Fijian land rights would be protected, and little land has been sold since. Of the 4½ million acres in Fiji about half a million are freehold, 50,000 Crown land under lease, and 312,000 native land under lease, mainly to Indian sugar farmers and Europeans. Native land is under the control of the Native Lands Trust Board and may not be sold.

Native Fijian agriculture is mainly concerned with the growing of root crops – taro, yams, manioc, kumara – as well as bananas, breadfruit, pawpaws, etc. Gardens or *tei-tei* are in the forest near the village. New clearings are made every year or two and work is often on a communal basis. Copra and bananas are the main commercial crops grown by Fijians, although a few grow sugar and tobacco.

The most important commercial crop is sugar, about 140,000 acres being grown by the South Pacific Sugar Mills, and Indian small farmers on leased land in the dry zone. European plantations produce about 40 per cent of the total copra.

Cattle ranching is carried out on the dry zone grasslands and there are several dairy farms in the wet zone.

### Exports:        Main Items 1965

| | | |
|---|---|---|
| Sugar | 305,166 tons | £12,287,986 |
| Copra, Coconut Oil, Coconut Meal | 26,499 tons | £2,438,917 |
| Gold | 112,432 ozs | £1,531,559 |
| Bananas (quarter of normal due to hurricane) | 50,527 cases | £67,741 |

Manganese, biscuits, hides, trochus shell and timber are also exported. Total export value was £21,016,861 in 1965.

**Industry:** The most important is sugar milling, carried out by the South Pacific Sugar Mills at Lautoka, Ba, Labasa, and Penang. Other important industries are gold mining at Vatukoula, manganese mining in western Viti Levu, and a coconut oil mill in Suva. Fijian copra is increasingly being milled here.

Other industries on a much smaller scale include manufacturing butter, biscuits, cigarettes, beer, clothing, ice cream, aerated waters, concrete pipes, soap, polished rice, and canning fish. Sawmilling, producing timber for houses, furniture, boat building, and fruitcases, is carried on in several areas.

**Towns:** Suva, with a population of about 55,000, is the capital and chief port. It is the main commercial and administrative centre.

Other important centres on Viti Levu are Lautoka, Vatukoula, Nausori, Ba. Labasa is the chief town on Vanua Levu. Levuka, the ancient capital of Fiji, is on Ovalau Island.

**Communications:** Fiji is a crossroads of the S.W. Pacific. Sea and air routes converge here from Australia, New Zealand, North America, and the Pacific Islands. Suva has a good port to accommodate large ships.

Nadi international airport can cater for all types of aircraft and has fine hotels. Some 90,000 passengers pass through Nadi in a year. Local air services join the three main islands and small vessels serve all the islands.

**Special Features:**
1. The tourist industry is growing in importance and is worth over £1 million annually.
2. The Fiji School of Medicine in Suva is a training centre for all islands in the S.W. Pacific.
3. A well-staffed department of agriculture makes Fiji a centre of agricultural progress in the Pacific.
4. There is a serious land problem. Indians form the major part of the population.

### Topographical Maps – Fiji

The two maps at the bottom of the opposite page are small sections of topographic maps of parts of Viti Levu in Fiji. They are on a scale of 1 : 50,000 or approximately one inch to four-fifths of a mile.

Because of the scale, these maps can show detail of the land 50 times greater than in the map at the top of the page. Very few of the Pacific Islands are mapped in as much detail.

The two maps show strongly contrasting types of landscape, as you will see if you study them, the map key and the following notes.

### Lautoka Area

Flattish coastal plain with some low hills (Tualesia 284 ft). Closely populated urban

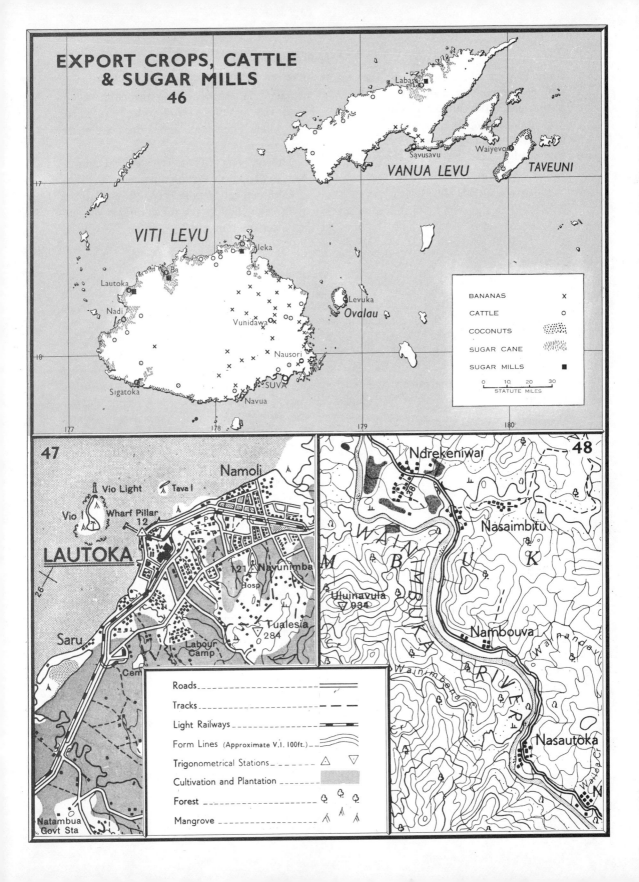

# EXPORT CROPS, CATTLE & SUGAR MILLS
## 46

**VANUA LEVU**

Labasa

Savusavu    Waiyevo    **TAVEUNI**

17

**VITI LEVU**

Tavaleka

Ba

Lautoka

Nadi

Vunidawa

Levuka
*Ovalau*

Nausori

18

SUVA

Sigatoka

Navua

| | |
|---|---|
| BANANAS | x |
| CATTLE | o |
| COCONUTS | |
| SUGAR CANE | |
| SUGAR MILLS | ■ |

0    10    20    30
STATUTE MILES

177    178    179    180

## 47

Namoli

Vio Light    Tava I

Vio I    Wharf Pillar
12

**LAUTOKA**

P

121  Navunimba

Hosp

Tualesia
284

Saru

Labour
Camp

Cem

Natambua
Govt Sta

## 48

Ndrekeniwai

38

Nasaimbitu

K

WAINIMBUKA

M

B

Uluinavula
934

Nambouva

Wainimbuka    RIVER

Wailoa Ck

Nasautoka

N

| | | |
|---|---|---|
| Roads | | ———— |
| Tracks | | – – – – |
| Light Railways | | ▬▬▬ |
| Form Lines (Approximate V.1. 100ft.) | | ≈ |
| Trigonometrical Stations | | △ ▽ |
| Cultivation and Plantation | | ▨ |
| Forest | | ♧ ♧ ♧ |
| Mangrove | | ⋏ ⋏ ⋏ |

area and port. Outside the town the land is well cultivated and mainly in small sugar plantations with scattered dwellings.

Communication is easy with roads, tracks and railways. The railways are for the transport of sugar cane to the mill, shown in black just inland from the wharf.

## Wainimbuka River Area

Typical of inland Viti Levu. River valley in an area of steep, rugged hills (Uluinavula 934 ft). Thinly populated area. Villages are situated on terraces along the river valley, with the exception of Ndrekeniwai where the valley opens out and slopes are more gentle.

The hills generally are forested and cultivation (*tei-tei*) is in scattered patches.

Communication is largely restricted to the river valley, i.e. to the road, or to boats and rafts on the river itself.

# NEW CALEDONIA

New Caledonia and its dependencies are a group of Melanesian islands situated in the Pacific Ocean between 164° 15′ and 167° 15′ W and 20° 8′ and 22° 25′ S. The island of New Caledonia lies about 1,115 miles east of Australia and about the same distance from the north-western extremity of New Zealand.

**Size and Physical Nature:** With its dependencies New Caledonia has an area of 7,335 sq. miles. It consists of the following sections:

| | |
|---|---|
| Island of New Caledonia (La Grande Terre) (250 miles long and 25 miles wide) | 6,530 sq. miles |
| Isle of Pines | 51.7 sq. miles |
| Loyalty Islands | 756 sq. miles |
| Huon Islands | Four small islets |

The island of New Caledonia is mountainous and broken, rising to 5,375 ft (Mt Panié, and Humboldt Peak 5,360 ft), with discontinuous parallel ranges, interior plateaux, a steep N.E. side and more gently sloping S.W. side. There are a number of small rivers with restricted alluvial flats. Consisting of metamorphic and sedimentary rocks, the island has rich mineral deposits. Off shore lies a barrier reef, the longest insular coral reef in the world.

**Government:** The inhabitants of New Caledonia and its dependencies are French citizens and enjoy universal suffrage. New Caledonia is an overseas territory of the French Republic and has direct representation in the French Parliament (one deputy and one senator, both elected). The Governor of New Caledonia is also High Commissioner for France in the Pacific and is responsible for the French interest in New Hebrides and French Oceania.

There is an elected assembly of 30 members. There is also a Council of Government consisting of six Ministers, a Vice-President, and the Governor as President.

**Population and Settlement:** The native people are Melanesian but make up only half of the total population. They are divided into tribes speaking different dialects, but all speak French.

There are many Europeans, mainly of French descent, Asians, and other Pacific Islanders who work chiefly as labourers.

### Population

| | 1850 | 1958 | 1964 |
|---|---|---|---|
| Melanesians | | 36,670 | 43,300 |
| Europeans | | 24,389 | 40,664 |
| Asians | | 7,700 | 4,200 |
| Others | | 670 | 680 |
| Total | 70,000 | 69,429 | 88,844 |

Density of Population 12 per sq. mile

The indigenous people live in villages on

native reserves, and in the towns. Their houses are mainly of cement or earth walls with thatched roofs, replacing the traditional bark-walled, beehive-shaped houses. Europeans live mainly on small coffee plantations, on ranches, and in the towns. About 15,000 Melanesians live in the Loyalty Islands.

**Climate and Vegetation:** New Caledonia lies in the zone of S.E. trade winds and because of its long rugged nature the winds bring abundant moisture only to eastern, southern, and higher parts.

| | | |
|---|---|---|
| Average annual rainfall | Noumea | 43" |
| | Yaté | 130" |
| Average temperature | Noumea (January) | 79° |
| | (July) | 69° |

June to November is a drier season. During the warm season (from the end of November to the end of March) the temperature seldom exceeds 95°F and during the cool season (from the end of March to the end of November) never falls below 40°F.

The damp eastern slopes above 1,200 ft are well forested with kauri, pines and hardwoods. Interior plateaux and the dry western side are covered with savannah and scattered *niaouli*, a eucalyptus-like shrub. Coastal areas are fringed with mangroves.

**Land Tenure and Farming:** Land is held by the state, which leases it out for farming and mining. Land is reserved for the native people. They grow yams, irrigated taro, manioc, maize, sweet potatoes, coffee, bananas, and coconuts in valley bottoms and on terraced hillsides. The Loyalty Islands people grow food crops, they fish, and make 75 per cent of the total copra. The main agricultural product is coffee. About 12,000 acres are grown, half by the natives and half on European plantations. Two varieties are grown, *Arabica* in the west and blight-resistant *Robusta* in the more humid east. Coffee grows at sea level in New

Caledonia and the coast from Canala to Hienghène is the most important area.

Maize, rice, potatoes, vegetables, and fruits are also grown.

One per cent of land is cultivated. About 25 per cent, particularly on the western side, is devoted to stock rearing. Europeans own 95 per cent of the cattle, mainly Shorthorn, French Limousin, and Hereford breeds. Poor pasture, weeds, ticks, and wild deer are problems.

**Exports:** 1963

| | Tons | Value* |
|---|---|---|
| Nickel Ore | 616,709 | 538,000 |
| Nickel Matte | 17,863 | 924,000 |
| Ferro Nickel | 29,468 | 300,700 |
| Chrome | 17,955 | 36,600 |
| Iron Ore | 283,810 | 65,500 |
| Coffee | 1,255 | 64,300 |
| Copra | 1,005 | 11,000 |
| Trochus Shell | 126 | 1,600 |
| Hides | 57 | 500 |

*Pacific francs, in thousands (125 frs = $NZ1)

**Industry:** Mining is by far the most important industry, accounting for over 90 per cent of exports. Nickel and chrome are most important though iron, manganese, cobalt, coal, and other minerals occur. The bulk of the chrome is produced at the Tiebaghi mine. Nickel comes from a score of small mines, but three-quarters comes from a huge open-cast on the plateau at Thio. Modern methods are used.

The nickel ore is smelted in works at Point Doniambo, near Noumea, using power from a hydro-electric station at Yaté.

A meat-packing plant at Ouaco and soap works are based on local products and there are some service industries.

**Towns:** Noumea is the capital and chief port. It is an attractive tree-shaded town of more than 35,000 people, with a good harbour. Three-fifths of the Europeans live here and it is the commercial, administrative, and industrial centre of New Caledonia. There are

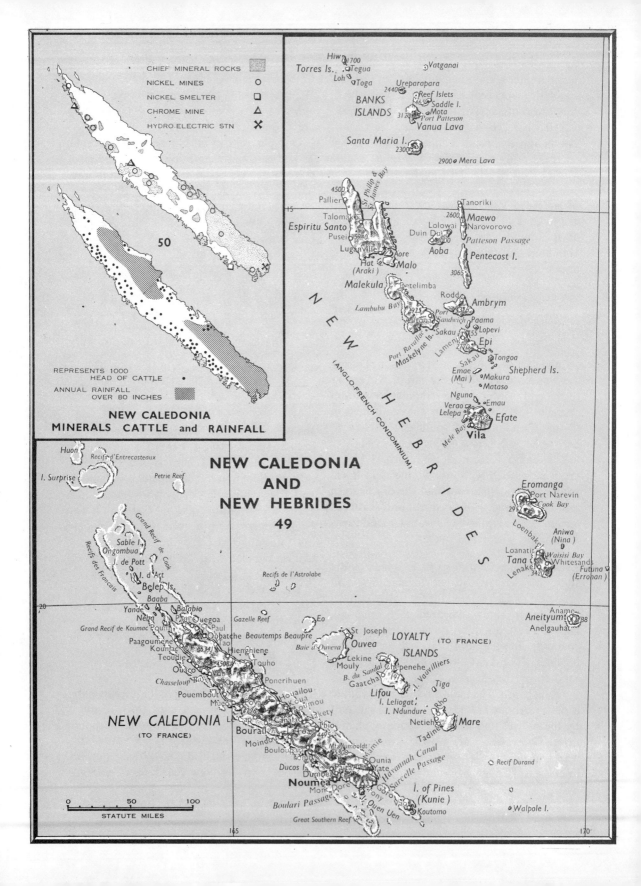

**CHIEF MINERAL ROCKS**
**NICKEL MINES** ○
**NICKEL SMELTER** □
**CHROME MINE** △
**HYDRO-ELECTRIC STN** ✕

50

REPRESENTS 1000
HEAD OF CATTLE ·
ANNUAL RAINFALL
OVER 80 INCHES

**NEW CALEDONIA**
**MINERALS CATTLE and RAINFALL**

Hiw 1700
Torres Is. Tegua
Loh Toga ⊙Vatganai
2440
BANKS Ureparapara
ISLANDS Reef Islets
1452 Saddle I.
Mota
3120 Port Patteson
Vanua Lava

Santa Maria I.
2300⊙

2900⊙ Mera Lava

St Philip & James Bay
4500
Pallier
Talomaco Tanoriki
Espiritu Santo 2600
Lolowai Maewo
Pusei 5980 Duin Dur Narovorovo
Luganville Patteson Passage
Aore
Hat ⊙Malo Aoba Pentecost I.
(Araki) 3065
Malekula Betelimba

Rodd
Lambubu Bay Ambrym
Port
Port Sandwich Paama
Aulua 2925 Sakau 1455 Lopevi
Port Ravallot Epi
Maskelyne Is. 2700
Sakau
Lamen Tongoa
Emae Makura Shepherd Is.
(Mai) Mataso

NEW Nguna Emau
Verao Emao
Lelepa 3203 Efate
Mele Bay Vila

HEBRIDES

(ANGLO-FRENCH CONDOMINIUM)

Eromanga
Port Narevin
295 Cook Bay

Loenbakel
Aniwa
(Nina)
Loanati
Tana Waisisi Bay
Lenake Whitesands
3420 Futuna
(Errohan)

Huon
Recifs d'Entrecasteaux
I. Surprise Petrie Reef

**NEW CALEDONIA**
**AND**
**NEW HEBRIDES**
**49**

Grand Recif de Cook
Sable I.
Ongombua
J. de Pott
I. d'Art
Recifs des Francais
Belep Is.
Recifs de l'Astrolabe
Baaba
Yande Balabio Gazelle Reef Eo
Nela Pum Ouegoa St Joseph LOYALTY (TO FRANCE)
Grand Recif de Koumac Poum Paul Beautemps Beaupre Ouvea ISLANDS
Paagoumene Oubatche Baie d'Ouvea Lekine
Koumac Tao Mouly Chepenehe
Teoudie 1634 Hienghiene Gaatcha 197 I. Vauvilliers
Ouaco 4508 Touho Lifou Tiga
Chasseloup Kone Ponerihuen Houailou I. Leliogat
Pouembout Koua I. Ndundure Rho
Muen Netieh Mare
NEW CALEDONIA Canala Thio Tadine
Bourail Mt Humboldt Recif Durand
Moindou 5308 Mamie
Bouloupari Ounia Yate
Ducos Mont Dore Mhavannah Canal Sarcelle Passage
Dumbea Goro
Noumea Tony Uen Uen I. of Pines Walpole I.
Boulari Passage Koutomo (Kunie)
Great Southern Reef

Aname
Aneityum 2788
Anelgauhat

NEW HEBRIDES

0 50 100
STATUTE MILES

several smaller centres of trade, mining, and shipping.

**Communications:** Shipping lines link Noumea with Australia, Fiji, North America, and Europe. A French airline and Qantas link New Caledonia with Australia, Fiji, New Zealand, North America, and Europe. The airport at Tontouta, 30 miles from Noumea, can accommodate jet aircraft. Local shipping and air services operate. There is a broadcasting and radio telephone service.

**Special Features:**

1. Noumea is the headquarters of the South Pacific Commission.
2. The tourist industry is growing in importance and earns over half a million dollars annually.
3. New Caledonia was originally a French penal settlement.

# NEW HEBRIDES

**Size and Physical Nature:** Area 5,700 sq. miles. About 80 islands of which all but 12 are small. Espiritu Santo (1,500 sq. miles) is the largest. The islands are mountainous (Mt Talwesamana on Santo over 6,150 ft, Santo peak over 6,000 ft) and volcanic, being the crests of a submarine ridge. Many have raised coral plateaux and cultivable coastal strips. There are four active volcanoes on Tana, Lopevi, and Ambrym.

**Government:** A *condominium* administered by both Great Britain and France. The two local heads of the Anglo-French *condominium* are the two Resident Commissioners at Port Vila. They are assisted by an Advisory Council including French, British, and New Hebridean members.

There are three sets of laws, three currencies (British, Australian, and French), and two kinds of weights and measurements.

French and English are both official languages. In addition many local people speak *bichelamar*, a dialect based on English which developed originally in ports where sailors, traders, and natives were accustomed to meet.

**Population and Settlement:** The native people are Melanesian and speak many different dialects. The inhabitants of the Banks and Torres Groups are Polynesian, as are those of several other small areas.

## Population (1964 est.)

| | |
|---|---|
| Native people | 61,550 |
| British subjects (citizens and British protected persons) | 1,068 (including 597 Europeans) |
| French subjects (citizens and French protected persons) | 3,178 (including 330 Vietnamese; 108 French protected persons) |
| Total | 65,796 |

## Population of Main Islands

| | | | |
|---|---|---|---|
| Tanna | 8,241 | Espiritu Santo | 6,200 |
| Erromango | 514 | Aoba | 5,514 |
| Efate | 5,410 | Banks Islands | 3,059 |
| Tongoa | 2,216 | Pentecost | 4,876 |
| Malekula | 9,207 | Ambrym | 3,670 |

The islands are thinly populated with a density of only 11 per sq. mile.

Native villages are often inland in the hills, because of the prevalence of malaria near sea level, but more than half the population live near the sea.

**Climate and Vegetation:** Annual average rainfall increases from about 90″ in the south to 150″ in the north (Vila annual average 91″). Average temperatures (Vila 72°–82°F monthly average) and average humidities (85° to 91°) are high. The S.E. trades moderate the climate between May and October. At other times cyclones may occur.

The large islands are densely forested, though the higher plateaux, especially on the leeward side, have a savannah-like vegetation. Kauri, pine, teak and sandalwood are plentiful.

**Land Tenure and Farming:** Land is native owned, but European planters cultivate land which they originally bought from native owners. Most of the population is engaged in agriculture. The native people practise a form of shifting cultivation and grow yams, taro, manioc, and breadfruit. They also produce 50 per cent of the total copra.

European plantations, situated on the coastal plains, mainly on Espiritu Santo, Pentecost, Malekula, and Efate, produce copra, cocoa, and coffee. Cattle are raised on these plantations.

The Vietnamese, Chinese, Tahitians, and Wallisians were brought in as labour on plantations, but many Vietnamese had returned to North Vietnam by the end of 1963. Native people are also employed

| Exports: | 1965 | |
|---|---|---|
| Copra | 28,726 tons | £1,893,000 |
| Cocoa | 514 tons | £44,700 |
| Manganese Ore | 79,384 tons | £839,000 |
| Frozen Fish | 3,336 tons | £392,600 |

**Industry:** The only industries are a factory on Santo for freezing tuna caught by Japanese boats on contract, timber milling, and open-cast mining of manganese at Forari on Efate (capacity of annual production 60,000 tons).

**Towns:** Port Vila (4,500) on Efate; the only other town is Luganville (3,600), on the Segond Channel on Espiritu Santo.

**Communications:** There are frequent and regular air and shipping services. Twice weekly air services link Vila and Luganville with Noumea and the outside world, and twice weekly services link Vila, Fiji, and the Solomons. Several shipping lines link the New Hebrides with Europe, other Pacific territories, and Australia.

Transport between the islands of the group is by small vessels and by local airways.

**Special Features:**
The New Hebrides are underdeveloped and malarial in some places, but are very fertile and have good possibilities.

# SOLOMON ISLANDS

**Size and Physical Nature:** Area 11,500 sq. miles. One of the largest groups in the Pacific.
Area of the largest islands:

| | |
|---|---|
| Guadalcanal | 2,500 sq. miles |
| Ysabel | 1,800 sq. miles |
| San Cristoval | 1,800 sq. miles |
| Malaita | 1,500 sq. miles |
| New Georgia | 1,300 sq. miles |
| Choiseul | 980 sq. miles |

The Lord Howe (Ontong Java), Santa Cruz, Duff, and Reef Groups are included in the territory.

The islands are mountainous, rising to 7,600 ft on Guadalcanal, heavily wooded, and well watered. There are some volcanoes; several smaller islands are of coral formation. There are ten large islands or groups of islands.

**Government:** The islands are a British Protectorate governed directly by the High Commissioner for the Western Pacific whose head-

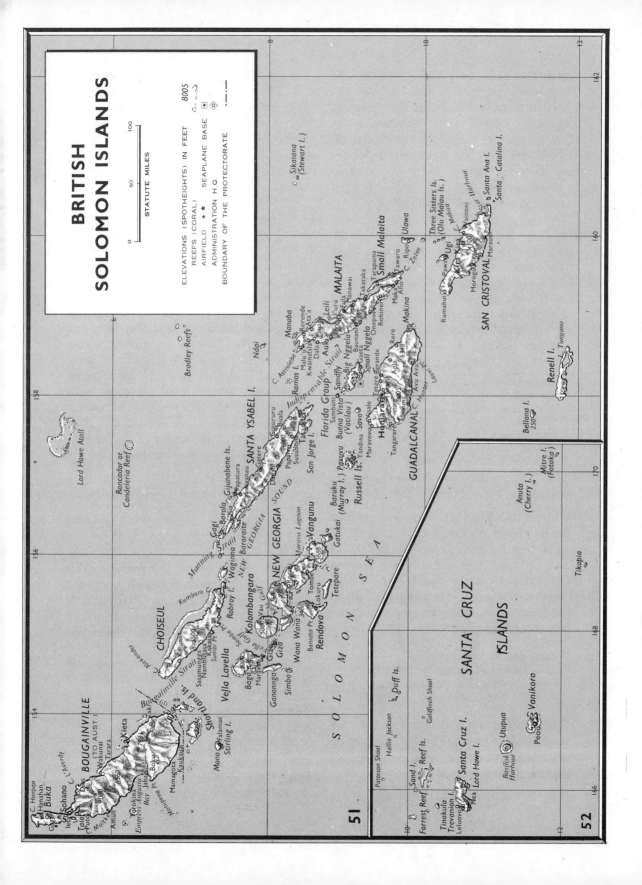

# BRITISH SOLOMON ISLANDS

STATUTE MILES

ELEVATIONS (SPOTHEIGHTS) IN FEET 8005
REEFS (CORAL)
AIRFIELD ✱ ★
ADMINISTRATION H.Q. SEAPLANE BASE
BOUNDARY OF THE PROTECTORATE ‑‑‑‑‑

51

52

C. Henpan
Hanahan
Buka
Gesan
leep Sohano
Talo C. L'Averdy
Puto
Kukunai
Wakunai
BOUGAINVILLE
(TO AUST.)
Kieta
Jabla
Toboroi
Empress Augusta Bay
Mamagota
Amun
Mono
Falamae Stirling I.
Shortland Is.
Buin Pt
Boku
Kukunai

Lord Howe Atoll

Roncador or
Candeleria Reef

Bradley Reefs

Ndai

Sikaiana
(Stewart I.)

SANTA YSABEL I.
Gagi
Gijunabene Is.
Barola
Pepatura
Kwanau
Gatere
Papatura
CHOISEUL
Manning Strait
Robroy I.
Wagina
Kumbora
Sepi
Nambikaka
Sasamungga
Sumbi Pt
C. Alexander
Baga
Gizo
Ganongga Grita
Wana Wana
Simbo
Marovo Lagoon
NEW GEORGIA
GEORGIA SOUND
Kolombangara
Vangunu
Rendova
Lokuru
Gatukai
Tetepare
Vella Lavella
Vella Gulf

Ramos
Manoba
Kerende
C. Astrolabe
Malu u
Kwai
Ata'a
Kwaikalala
Dala
Auki
Langa Langa
Leili
MALAITA
Faua
Nafinua
Tarapaina
Small MALAITA
Tarapaina
Takataka
Rohinari
Ulawa
Tawaro
C. Zelee
Maka
Alito
Apio
Makina

Florida Group
Sambeni
Sandfly I.
Buena Vista
(Vatilau)
Savo
Russell Is.
Baruku
Paguyu
(Murray I.)
Maravovo
Vale
Tangarare
Yandina
Honiara
Tetere Brande
Aola
Avu Avu
C. Hunter
GUADALCANAL
Small Nggela
Big Nggela
Baunani
Gaeta

Bellona I.
250

Renell I.
Tungano

Three Sisters Is.
(Olu Malau Is.)
Rumahui
Pawo
Ugi
Mohua
Ugi
Moroguo
Nainoni
SAN CRISTOVAL
Maraun
Santa Ana I.
Santa Catalina I.

SOLOMON SEA

Patteson Shoal
Hallie Jackson
Duff Is.
Sand I.
Forrest Reef
Reef Is.
Tinakula
Trevanion I.
Leluovai
Nea Lord Howe I.
Santa Cruz I.
Utupua
Basilisk Harbour
Peou
Vanikoro

SANTA CRUZ
ISLANDS

Tikopia

Anuta
(Cherry I.)

Mitre I.
(Fataka)

quarters are at Honiara on Guadalcanal. The protectorate is divided into four districts under District Commissioners. Executive and Legislative Councils (21 members, eight elected, and 10 members, four elected, respectively) carry out legislation under the High Commissioner.

Local matters are dealt with by local courts and elected local councils.

**Population and Settlement:** The native people are mainly Melanesians, though they vary in type. Those on the islands of Ontong Java, Sikaiana, Rennell, Bellona, the Reef Group, and Tikopia are Polynesian in type. The people have a tribal system with a headman, but no hereditary chiefs. Many dialects are spoken.

|              | 1959 (census) | 1965    |
|--------------|---------------|---------|
| Melanesians  | 117,600       | 130,765 |
| Polynesians  | 4,600         | 5,180   |
| Europeans    | 780           | 1,120   |
| Chinese      | 340           | 510     |
| Micronesians | 460           | 1,840   |
| Others       | 220           | 255     |
| Total        | 124,000       | 139,670 |

Density of Population 12 per sq. mile
Rate of Increase 0.4%

Some 20,000 people, including most of the Europeans, live on Guadalcanal, 50,000 on Malaita, 8,000 on Santa Ysabel, 7,000 on San Cristoval, and about 6,000 each on Choiseul and Vella Lavella.

Native villages are both inland and coastal. European settlement on copra plantations is largely confined to narrow coastal lowlands.

**Climate and Vegetation:**

| Average annual rainfall | Tulagi 123″ |
|---|---|
| Average temperature (January) | Tulagi 82°F |
| Average temperature (July) | Tulagi 81°F |

May to October is the season of the S.E. trade winds and tends to be drier than the rest of the year. Rainfall is higher on the eastern coasts and increases with height.

Temperatures are high throughout the year and occasional hurricanes cause damage.

The large islands of the Solomons have a much greater variety, both in plants and animals, than islands further east in the Pacific. Most of the land is forested and pigs, rats, bats, many birds, crocodiles, and insects abound.

**Land Tenure and Farming:** The native people own 96 per cent of the land. The land is held by kinship groups and is divided, as in other parts of Melanesia, into bush, garden, and village land. In the bushland wild crops such as almonds and nuts from the sago palm are gathered, and wild pigs and birds are hunted. Garden land is cleared from the bush, and yams, taro, and bananas are grown. Village plots are close to village houses and grow food crops, breadfruit, coconuts, and tobacco.

European agriculture is concerned with coastal copra plantations run by individuals and by companies such as Lever Bros. Copra is the mainstay of the economy. Native production is increasing in importance.

| **Exports:** | **1961** | **1965** |
|---|---|---|
| Total value | £A1,866,484 | £A2,379,067 |
| Copra | 26,000 tons | 24,500 tons |
| Timber | 152,596 cubic feet | 687,936 cubic feet |
| Trochus Shell | 6,800 cwts | 2,946 cwts |
| Cocoa | | 75 tons |

**Industry:** Several timber companies operate and further milling concessions are being sought. Gold mining on a small scale is undertaken at Gold Ridge on Guadalcanal. There are soft drink factories in Honiara and a biscuit factory.

Manganese and various phosphates have been proved and will be mined.

**Towns:** Honiara (5,500 Solomon Islanders, 400 Chinese, 600 Europeans) on Guadalcanal is the capital and main settlement and now the centre of British administration for the Western Pacific.

Auki on Malaita, Gizo in the New Georgia Group and Kira Kira on San Cristoval are other main centres and have Government hospitals.

**Communications:** The Solomons are not well served by shipping. Passenger and cargo vessels call irregularly or infrequently. Air services connect with Australia, New Guinea, New Hebrides and Fiji. There are few roads on the islands and lack of transport is a major problem. There are radio facilities.

**Special Features:**

1. The Solomons are probably the most underpopulated of all the Pacific Islands.
2. The islands were of great strategic importance during World War II.
3. The islands are malarial.
4. Both health measures and education are now progressing fairly quickly.
5. UNESCO and the South Pacific Commission have established schools of printing, fisheries, and boat building in the group.

# NEW GUINEA

**Size and Physical Nature:** Total area 342,149 sq. miles (three and a third times the size of New Zealand), divided into Irian (Indonesian West New Guinea), Papua, and Australian New Guinea.

*West Irian*

Mainland (151,789 sq. miles). Includes the Schouten Islands (6,760 sq. miles). Total: 158,549 sq. miles

*Papua*

Mainland (87,806 sq. miles). Includes the islands of the Trobriands, Woodlark, D'Entrecasteaux, and Louisiade groups (2,794 sq. miles). Total: 90,600 sq. miles.

*Australian New Guinea*

Mainland (70,200 sq. miles). Includes Bismarck Archipelago (18,700 sq. miles) and Bougainville and Buka (4,100 sq. miles) of the Solomon Islands. Total: 93,000 sq. miles.

New Guinea is mountainous; much of it is inaccessible and unexplored. Two distinct series of mountain ranges run from east to west. Narrow coastal ranges in the north rise to 7,000 ft and are paralleled by a line of active volcanoes. These ranges are separated from the main central range by a depression in which lie the valleys of the Markham, Ramu, Sepik, and Mamberamo rivers. South of the rugged central ranges which rise to snow-capped peaks (Carstenz Toppen, 16,400 ft), lies an extensive lowland across which flow several large rivers with their swampy deltas.

**Government:** West New Guinea (Irian Barat), formerly part of the Netherlands East Indies, came under the control of Indonesia in 1962.

Eastern New Guinea consists of two political units, the territory of Papua and the United Nations Trusteeship territory of New Guinea. Both units are administered by Australia under the Papua and New Guinea Act. The Legislative Council consists of the Administrator, 14 official members (either natives or non-natives), 12 elected members (six natives and six non-natives), and ten nominated members (at least five natives).

Papua is divided into six and New Guinea into nine districts for local administration.

**Population and Settlement:** The native peoples are varied in racial character, from the Negritoid pygmy tribes of the interior to Australoids in the south-east and Melanesians in the east and coastal areas. Many languages and dialects are spoken. The native peoples live in tribes, many of which in remote areas have a simple, stone-age culture.

## Population

Estimated total for New Guinea as a whole, 2,900,000 (1964)

|                | Irian (1959) | Papua (1964) | Aust. New Guinea (1964) |
|----------------|-------------|-------------|-------------------------|
| Indigenous     | 709,000     | 548,852     | 1,522,156               |
| Non-indigenous | 33,000      | 12,888      | 16,920                  |
| Total          | 742,000     | 561,740     | 1,539,076               |

## Non-indigenous composition

|          | Irian (1959) | Papua (1961) | Aust. New Guinea (1961) |
|----------|-------------|-------------|-------------------------|
| European | 16,000      | 8,260       | 11,702                  |
| Asian    | 17,000      | 106         | 2,545                   |
| Others   |             | 1,428       | 1,289                   |

Rate of Increase 2.5%

42 % of the population are under 14 years of age.

The main concentration of settlement is in the valleys and plateaux of the central highlands. European settlement is mainly confined to the town centres, plantations, and to the mining and sawmilling centres. Almost 100,000 natives now work for wages in various capacities. By May 1962 most of the 16,000 Europeans, who were Dutch, had left Irian. No census has ever been carried out in the central highlands, and estimates of native population there are approximate.

### Climate and Vegetation:

|                       | Kikori (Papua) | Port Moresby |
|-----------------------|----------------|--------------|
| Average annual rainfall | 231″         | 40″          |

There are two "seasons": one from May to October, when the south-east trade winds dominate, making the southern and eastern sides wetter; and the other from December to March, when the north-west monsoons prevail. Exposure to rain-bearing winds causes great variation in rainfall.

There is a wide temperature range because of differences in altitude. Temperatures of 100°F (maximum along the coast) vary to freezing point (on high mountain peaks).

Most of New Guinea is covered in tropical rain forest which contains valuable timbers, though difficult of access. Drier areas are covered in savannah or reed grasses. Poorly drained deltas and coastal lowlands have swamp plants and sago palms. The coast is fringed with mangroves, pandanus, and coconut.

**Land Tenure and Farming:** The normal rights of ownership are acquired by birth to a land-holding group. There is now some buying and selling of land among natives. Non-natives may lease new land only through the administration.

Native farming is mainly subsistence, based on shifting agriculture and "bush fallow". Individual or family plots are scattered from near the village to several miles away from it. Depending on the soil and altitude, yams, taro, sweet potato, coconuts, bananas, pawpaws, maize, sugar cane, cassava, peanuts, rice, and tobacco are grown. In swampy low-lying areas, the sago palm is the staple food. Natives produce about 25 per cent of the copra. Fishing and hunting are important.

European farming is concerned with coconut, rubber, tea, cocoa, and coffee plantations, and with limited stock raising in the highlands.

### Exports:     1964 (£'s Australian)

|                        | Papua     | New Guinea |
|------------------------|-----------|------------|
| Copra                  | 983,805   | 4,025,153  |
| Other Coconut Products |           | 594,725    |
| Rubber                 | 1,217,000 | 9,083      |
| Cocoa Beans            | 49,761    | 3,371,705  |
| Coffee Beans           | 20,100    | 2,662,821  |
| Peanuts                |           | 286,360    |

(Continued overleaf)

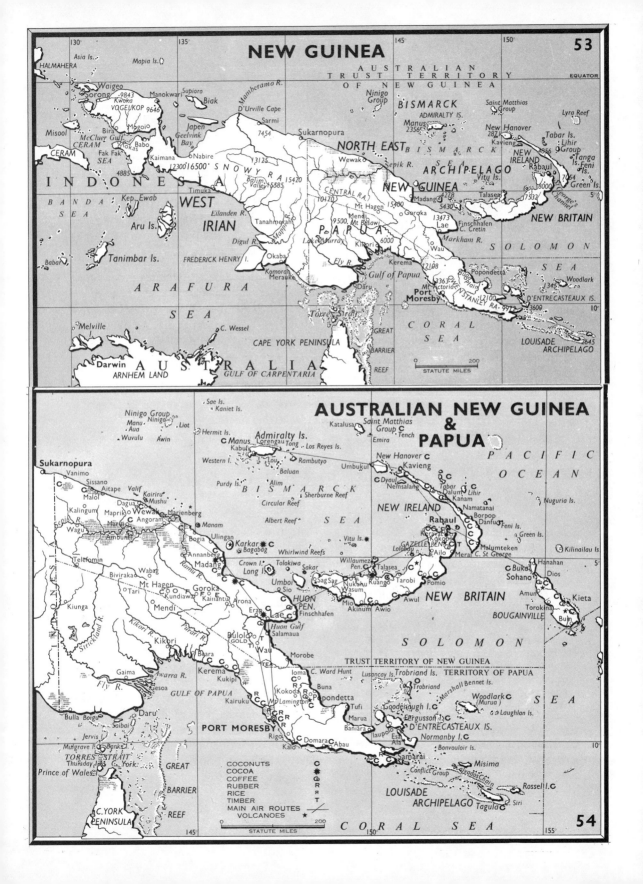

**Exports 1964** *(Continued)*

|  | *Papua* | *New Guinea* |
|---|---|---|
| Gold | 446 | 659,760 |
| Shell | 12,230 | 38,320 |
| Timber | 60,710 | 664,320 |
| Plywood | 474 | 974,199 |
| Veneer |  | 34,164 |
| Crocodile Skins | 264,337 | 188,414 |
| Other | 50,188 | 38,414 |
| Total (£'s Australian) | 2,659,051 | 13,547,438 |

**Industry:** Mostly concerned with processing primary products for export. Most important is the copra crushing mill near Rabaul, and a plywood and veneer factory at Bulolo. Nearly 50 sawmills are in operation, and there are factories producing paint, tobacco, biscuits, soft drink, beer, and tea. The building industry is well serviced by joinery, metal, and concrete factories.

Although many minerals exist only gold and its associated silver have been mined. The most important field is in the alluvial valleys of the Morobe district. Oil is mined in the Vogelkop area of West New Guinea and prospecting is going on in other areas.

**Towns:** Port Moresby (31,000) is the administrative capital of Papua-New Guinea. The main ports otherwise are Lae (8,000), Madang (4,000), Rabaul (9,000), Wewak, Kavieng, Lorengau, and Kieta. Chief inland centres are Bulolo and Wau. In Irian Sukarnopura (formerly Hollandia), Manokwari, Fakfak, Kaimana, Merauke and Wamena are the main settlements.

**Communications:** Large steamers service the chief ports and small craft ply coastwise. There are roads around the towns but only two "trunk" roads, from Lae to Wau and from Lae through the Markham valley.

Air services are immensely important in New Guinea. Air lines connect it with Australia and with Indonesia. Many small airports and airstrips serve the settlements and outlying districts.

# GILBERT AND ELLICE ISLANDS
## AND NAURU ISLAND

**Size and Physical Nature:** Area 369 sq. miles scattered over a million sq. miles of ocean. Thirty-seven islands, all of which are low coral islands or atolls no more than 15 ft high. Ocean Island is a raised coral island.

The islands consist of:

| | | |
|---|---|---|
| The Gilbert group | 16 islands | 114 sq. miles |
| The Ellice group | 9 islands | 10 sq. miles |
| The Phoenix group | 8 islands | 11 sq. miles |
| The Line group: | | |
|   Christmas Island | | 222 sq. miles |
|   Fanning Island | | 12½ sq. miles |
|   Washington Island | | 3 sq. miles |
| Ocean Island | | 2½ sq. miles |

**Government:** The islands form a British Crown Colony administered through the High Commissioner for the Western Pacific.

There is a resident commissioner at Tarawa Island assisted by an Advisory Council and an Executive Council. Each island has an Island Council which makes local laws.

**Population and Settlement:** The Gilbertese are Micronesians while the Ellice people are Polynesians.

Tarawa Island in the Gilberts has the largest population with 9,000 people, and a population density of 1,000 per sq. mile. In spite of dry sandy soil, most of these flat islands are densely populated (overall density 135 per sq. mile). Most people live in villages which are often ribbon-like and on the lagoon side of the islets; houses have a raised floor and open sides. Most villages have a church

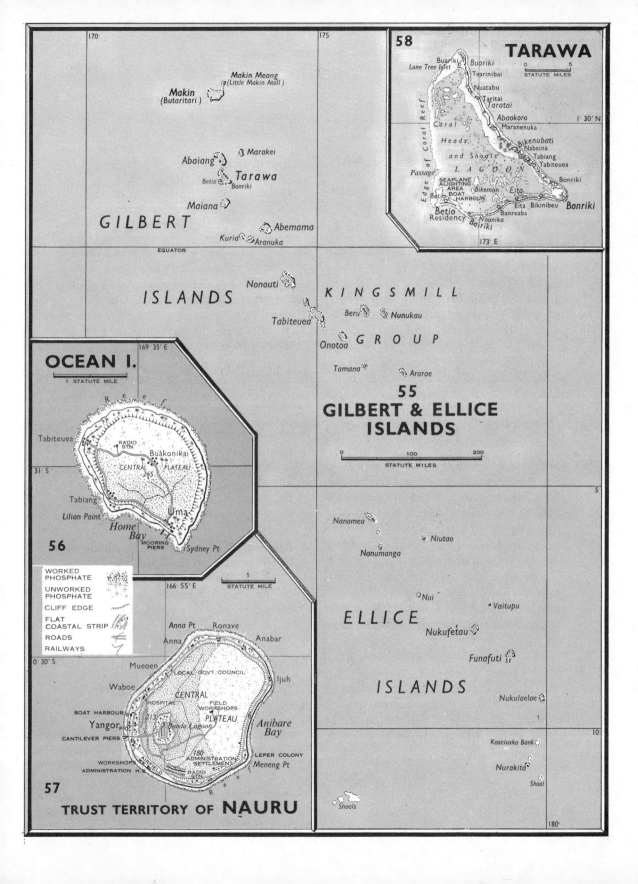

and a school. Betio settlement on Tarawa has 3,000 people.

### Population (1963)

| | |
|---|---|
| Gilbert | 37,319 (654 Europeans and others) |
| Ellice | 5,107 (337 Europeans and others) |
| Phoenix | 1,015 (3 Europeans and others) |
| Line | 1,329 (42 Europeans) |
| Ocean Island | 2,458 (248 Europeans and Chinese) |

Total 52,000 (1966)

Rate of Increase 3%

**Climate and Vegetation:** Rainfall varies widely from island to island and from year to year. Annual average rainfall varies from 40″ at the equator to 120″ in the islands furthest north and south. Yearly variation on Tarawa is 15″ to 138″. Droughts are common. Temperatures average 83° at Tarawa and become lower N. and S., but are never lower than 70°. Being astride the equator they lie in the doldrums, but both N.E. and S.E. trades blow seasonally as the sun moves north and south.

Coconuts and pandanus (screw pine) are the dominant vegetation.

**Land Tenure and Farming:** Apart from the Line Islands which are leased for coconut plantations, all land is owned and used by the native people. After his death land passes to an owner's next of kin. Because of subdivision among next of kin, many farms are less than a quarter of an acre in size.

In the thin sandy soils the range of crops grown is small. *Babai*, a kind of taro, is grown in artificial pits. Coconuts, flour from the pandanus fruit, bananas, and fish from

reef, lagoon, and sea are other important foods.

**Exports:** Copra for export (7,000 tons, 1965, valued at $A1 million) is produced on all islands and shipped to Tarawa. More important is the export of phosphate from Ocean Island (300,000 tons, $A13¼ million, 1965).

**Communications:** Communication with the outside world is poor. Phosphate ships maintain a fairly frequent service between Australia and New Zealand and Ocean Island. Copra ships make irregular calls at Tarawa. Inter-island communication is by small Government vessels. These belong to the Wholesale Society Co-operative, but are at the disposal of the Government. Air services are even less frequent. There is a regular weekly air service from Fiji to Funafuti and Tarawa, where there is an airstrip built during World War II.

**Special Features:**

1. Canton Island in the Phoenix group lies halfway between Honolulu and Noumea. Until recently it was an important stopover for transpacific planes. With the advent of long-range aircraft it has become an emergency airstrip.
2. Fanning Island is a connecting link in the Pacific cable between Canada and Fiji.
3. Christmas Island has been used since 1956 by the United Kingdom for nuclear experiments and was the site of nuclear bomb tests.

## NAURU ISLAND

Like Ocean Island, Nauru is an oval raised coral island, the centre containing rich deposits of phosphate of lime formed in the ancient lagoon. With an area of 8½ sq. miles, it is a United Nations trusteeship territory with an Australian administrator.

Population (1966): 6,048 (2,921 Nauruans, 1,532 other islanders, 1,167 Chinese, 428 Europeans).

The Nauruans live in villages situated on a narrow flat coastal terrace and by a small central lake.

The Europeans, Chinese, and other islanders are concerned in mining phosphate. This is carried out by open-cast methods under the control of the British Phosphate Commissioners. Phosphate is treated and exported from Yangor, the chief settlement, to Australia, New Zealand, and Great Britain.

The Nauruans receive royalties for phosphate mined. They are at present purchasing the phosphate plant and will completely control the plant by 1970. They will also have independence in 1968.

**Exports:**

**Tons of Phosphate Exported**

| Date | Nauru | Ocean |
|------|-------|-------|
| 1935 | 480,950 | 281,280 |
| 1952 | 1,061,797 | 281,762 |
| 1966 | 1,532,650 | 300,000 (approx.) |

# UNITED STATES TRUST TERRITORY
## AND GUAM

**Size and Physical Nature:** The trust territory consists of three archipelagoes – the Carolines, Marianas, and Marshalls. There are 2,141 small islands with a total land area of 700 sq. miles scattered over an ocean area of 3,000,000 sq. miles. Only 96 islands are inhabited.

The Marshalls and the Carolines, with the exception of Truk, Ponape, and Kusaie, are low coral islands and atolls; the Marianas are volcanic high islands.

**Government:** The territory is administered by the United States under the United Nations Trusteeship agreement. The headquarters of the High Commissioner are at Saipan. There are district administrators in the various districts, and elected councils in each district whose resolutions become law upon approval of the High Commissioner.

**Population and Settlement:** The people are Micronesians with the exception of the people of Kapingamarangi and Nukuoro, who are Polynesians.

The people are village dwellers, the atoll villages being linear in shape. Houses are traditionally of thatch with, in the Carolines, stone platforms. There is wide variety in housing, the larger islands having many of European style in wood or fibrolite and with iron roofs, originally encouraged by the Japanese.

**Population**

| 1937 | 50,741 |
|------|--------|
| 1954 | 61,102 |
| 1961 | 77,913 |
| 1966 | 92,373 |

The six districts have the following population (1966):

| | |
|---|---|
| Truk | 26,602 |
| Ponape | 18,958 |
| Marshall Islands | 18,239 |
| Palau | 11,225 |
| Mariana Islands | 10,743 |
| Yap | 6,606 |

Rate of Increase 3%

**Climate and Vegetation:** The islands have a tropical rainy climate with small seasonal changes.

Average annual rainfall varies from 90″ in the northern Marianas to 180″ in parts of the eastern Carolines.

Temperatures average 70°-85° in the Marianas, and 79°-92° in the Carolines and Marshalls. The islands are affected by monsoonal conditions and are subject to typhoons between August and January. Malaria is absent.

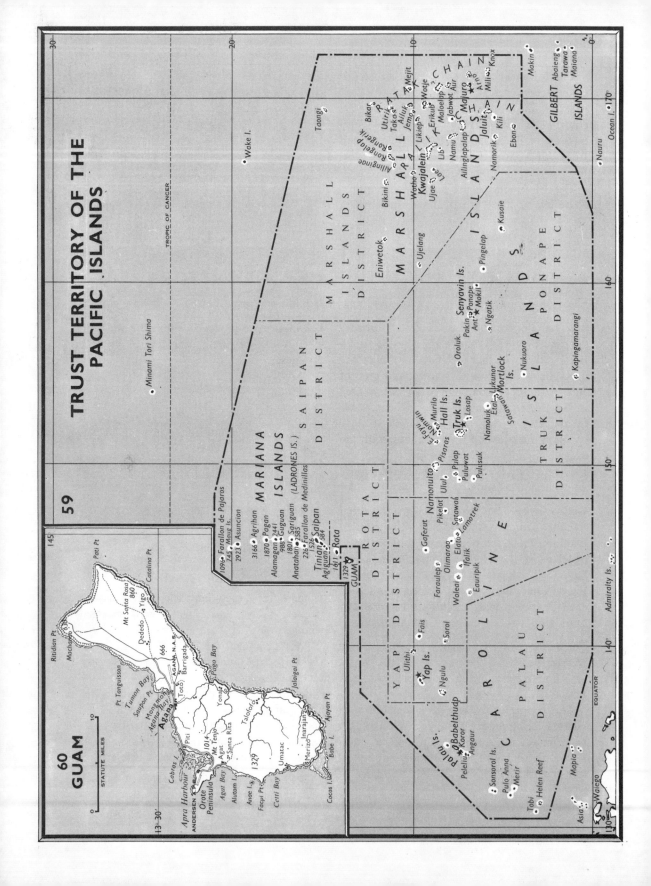

# TRUST TERRITORY OF THE PACIFIC ISLANDS

59

## GUAM

60

STATUTE MILES

MARIANA ISLANDS (LADRONES IS.)

SAIPAN DISTRICT

ROTA DISTRICT

YAP DISTRICT

PALAU DISTRICT

C A R O L I N E   I S L A N D S

TRUK DISTRICT

PONAPE DISTRICT

MARSHALL ISLANDS DISTRICT

R A T A K   C H A I N

R A L I K   C H A I N

M A R S H A L L   I S L A N D S

GILBERT ISLANDS

TROPIC OF CANCER

EQUATOR

Wake I.

Minami Tori Shima

Taongi

Farallon de Pajaros 1094
Maug Is. 745
Asuncion 2923
Agrihan 3166
Pagan 1870
Alamagan 2441
Guguan 988
Sariguan 1801
Anatahan 2585
Farallon de Medinillas 226
Saipan 1526
Tinian 584
Aguijan 611
Rota 1329

Bikar
Bikini
Eniwetok
Ujelang
Rongelap
Rongerik
Ailinginae
Wotho
Ujae
Lae
Kwajalein
Namu
Ailinglapalap
Jabwot
Namorik
Ebon
Kili
Jaluit
Namorik
Utirik
Taka
Ailuk
Jemo
Likiep
Erikub
Maloelap
Wotje
Mejit
Jabwot Aur
Majuro
Arno
Mili
Knox

Makin
Abaieng
Tarawa
Maiana

Nauru
Ocean I.

Kusaie
Ujelang
Senyavin Is.
Pakin Ponape
Ant Mokil
Pingelap
Ngatik
Oroluk
Nukuoro
Kapingamarangi

Hall Is.
Murilo
Nomwin
Fayu
Nomuin
Pisaras
Truk Is.
Losap
Namoluk
Etal Lukunor
Satowal Mortlock
Is.

Namonuito
Gaferut
Pikelot
Pulap
Puluwat
Pulusuk
Ulul
Satowal
Lamotrek
Elato
Ifalik
Faraulep
Olimarao
Woleai
Eauripik

Fais
Sorol
Ulithi
Yap Is.
Ngulu

Babelthuap
Koror
Peleliu
Angaur
Palau Is.

Sonsorol Is.
Pulo Anna
Merir
Tobi
Helen Reef

Mapia

Asia
Wateo

Admiralty Is.

---

### GUAM

Ritidian Pt.
Pati Pt.
Machanao 630
Mt. Santa Rosa 860
Yigo
Dededo 666
Pt. Tanguisson
Tumon Bay
Catalina Pt.
Barrigada
AGANA N.A.S.
ANDERSEN A.F.B.
Saupon Pt.
Mongmong
Agana Bay
AGANA
Piti
Cabras I.
Apra Harbour
Orote Peninsula
Agat Bay
Agat
Santa Rita
Mt. Tenjo 1014
Yona
Pago Bay
Toto
Talofofo
1329
Umatac
Merizo
Inarajan
Ajayan Pt.
Jalaigai Pt.
Talofofo Pt.
Anae I.
Alutom I.
Facpi Pt.
Cetti Bay
Cocos I.
Babe I.

Apart from the usual tropical island vegetation, hardwood forests occur in upland areas.

**Land Tenure and Farming:** Land is held by family groups. There is considerable variation in soil fertility, the high islands being more fertile. Native farming is mainly subsistence, depending on taro, yam, manioc, breadfruit, and banana. Coconuts are very important both for food and copra.

Under United States administration, agriculture and cattle raising is being encouraged and a "homesteading" system allows for new land to be developed and improved.

Fishing provides an important supplement to diet and fishermen's co-operatives export fish.

**Exports:** Copra represents over 90 per cent of export income.

### 1966

| | Weight | Value |
|---|---|---|
| Copra | 13,804 tons | $2,512,000 |
| Fish and Crab | | $78,102 |
| Trochus Shell | 431 tons | $71,483 |
| Vegetables | 295,277 lbs | $19,811 |
| Handicrafts | | $88,512 |
| Scrap Metal (World War II remnants) | 3,781 tons | $237,869 |

**Industry:** Handicrafts and fisheries are the only industries.

**Towns:** There is a main centre in each district (see stars, ★, on map). Saipan (8,664) in the Marianas is the largest.

**Communications:** A small fleet of vessels runs between Guam and the districts and also among the islands in the districts. No outside steamer service operates. The districts have a weekly air service.

**Special Features:**

1. Between World War I and World War II the territory was administered by the Japanese. They developed a substantial sugar industry on Saipan and neighbouring islands. Destroyed during World War II, the industry has not been revived.
2. The Marianas Trench, 37,800 ft deep, is the deepest part of the Pacific Ocean.
3. The islands are very important strategically and were the scenes of great battles during World War II.
4. Bikini atoll and Eniwetok atoll were the sites of early United States atom bomb tests, and the area has since been used for nuclear testing.

## GUAM

Guam (209 sq. miles; pop. 49,771 in 1966, plus 35,000 military) is the largest island between Hawaii and the Philippines and is not part of the Trust Territory. Guamanians are citizens of the United States though ineligible to vote in United States elections. There is a Governor and a locally elected legislature. Guam is a volcanic island with a rolling plain in the north and hilly savannah land in the south.

The economy is largely concerned with servicing the large military and naval base at Agana the capital, a modern city. Agriculture is limited and concerned mainly with producing food for local consumption and for the service base. Carabao (water buffalo) are used for cultivating.

Villages are now mainly of frame construction. The indigenous people (41,280 in 1966) are Chamorro stock with dominant outside strains.

Guam is well served by communications, two major shipping lines calling twice a week and two major airlines ten times weekly.

# PHILIPPINE ISLANDS

**Size and Physical Nature:** Area 115,600 sq. miles (ten times the size of the Solomon Islands and slightly larger than New Zealand). Consists of more than 7,000 islands in an archipelago which is 1,150 miles from north to south and 680 miles from east to west.

The main islands are:

| | sq. miles | | sq. miles |
|---|---|---|---|
| Luzon | 40,420 | Mindoro | 3,757 |
| Mindanao | 36,527 | Leyte | 2,785 |
| Samar | 5,049 | Cebu | 1,702 |
| Negros | 4,904 | Bohol | 1,492 |
| Palawan | 4,549 | Masbate | 1,262 |
| Panay | 4,445 | | |

The islands are mountainous (Mt Pulog 9,593 ft in Luzon, Mt Apo 9,690 ft in Mindanao), being part of the fold mountain arc running from Indonesia to Japan. Earthquakes and volcanoes are common. There are several large lakes. Rivers are short and swift.

**Government:** The Philippines have been an independent state since 1946. Conquered by the Spanish in 1565, the islands came under the rule of the U.S.A. in 1899. Both Spanish and American influences have affected Filipino culture.

The country is divided into 57 provinces, 39 chartered cities (directly under the central government), 983 municipalities, and 18,859 wards or districts (barrios).

**Population and Settlement:** The people are very mixed in race, religion and language. Most "Filipinos" are of Malay origin with a mixture of Chinese and Spanish. Eighty per cent are Roman Catholics, four per cent Moslems. There are more than 80 languages, of which the official ones are English, Tagolog (spoken around Manila), and Spanish.

### Population

| | |
|---|---|
| 1899 | 7,000,000 |
| 1939 | 16,000,000 |
| 1961 | 27,000,000 |
| 1966 | 33,470,000 |

Density of population 290 per sq. mile

The population is concentrated largely in two areas, the central plain of Luzon and the narrow lowlands around the coasts of the Visayan Islands, especially on the island of Cebu.

Filipinos live in scattered homesteads, in straggling villages (barrios) and in towns and cities. The common type of house has a gabled roof and is raised a few feet off the ground on posts. Building materials vary from bamboo with palm thatch to the increasingly popular frame house with sheet iron roof. There is wide variation in house construction. Towns have piped water and electricity, rural areas rarely.

There is an extensive system of schools and universities.

### Climate and Vegetation:

| | | | | |
|---|---|---|---|---|
| Average annual rainfall | Manila (west) | 82″ | Paracole (east) | 145″ |
| Average monthly temperature | Manila (north) | 80° | Davao (south) | 81° |

The islands lie in the monsoon area. The south-west monsoon brings heavy rain in summer. Western parts have a dry season in winter but eastern parts get rain then, also from the north-east trades, and have no dry season. Mindanao has rain the year round. Typhoons occur fairly frequently.

The hot wet climate encourages luxuriant plant growth. About 60 per cent of the country is in forest – tropical rain forest on lowlands and foothills, deciduous forest on higher slopes, and pine trees on mountains of central Luzon. In coastal areas mangroves, nipa palm and coconuts flourish. In drier

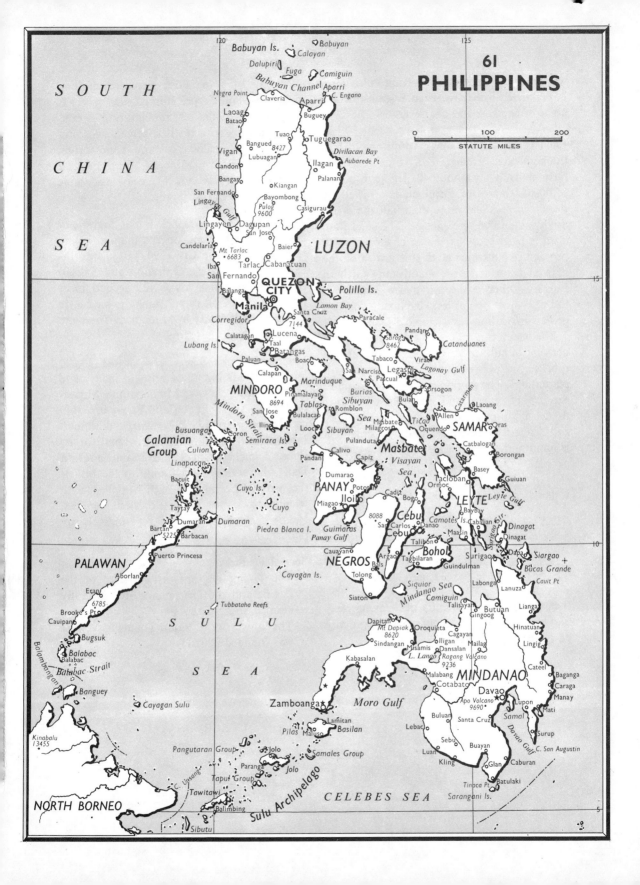

# PHILIPPINES

SOUTH

CHINA

SEA

STATUTE MILES

0    100    200

Babuyan Is.  ◦Babuyan
Dalupiri  ◦Calayan
Fuga  ◦Camiguin
Babuyan Channel  Aparri
Negra Point  Claveria  Aparri  C. Engano
Laoag
Bataac  Buguey
Vigan  Bangued  Tuao  Tuguegarao
8427
Candon  Lubuagan  Divilacan Bay
Bangar  Ilagan  Aubarede Pt
Kiangan  Palanan
San Fernando  Bayombong
Lingayen  Pulog  Casiguran
9600
Lingayen Gulf  Dagupan
San Jose
Candelaria  Baler
Mt Tarlac  LUZON
6683
Iba  Tarlac  Cabanatuan
San Fernando
Balanga  QUEZON  Polillo Is.
CITY
Manila  Lamon Bay
Corregidor  Santa Cruz  Paracale
7144  Lucena  Pandan
Calatagan  Taal  Sorog  Catanduanes
Lubang Is.  Batangas  Tabaco  8462
Paluan  Boac  San Narciso  Viras
Calapan  Marinduque  Pasual  Legaspi  Lagonay Gulf
MINDORO  Pinamalayan  Burias  Sorsogon
8694  Tablas  Sibuyan  Bulan
San Jose  Bulalacan  Romblon  Laoang
Iling  Looc  Sibuyan  Masbate  Ticao  Allen  SAMAR
Sea  Milagros  Oquendo  Oras
Busuanga  Semirara Is.  Sibuyan  Pulanduta  Catbalogan
Coron  Calivo  Capiz  Masbate  Borongan
Calamian  Culion  Pandan  Visayan  Basey
Group  Sea  Guiuan
Linapacan  Dumarao  Tacloban
Bacuit  Iloilo  Potoran  Ormoc  LEYTE  Leyte Gulf
Taytay  PANAY  Cadiz  Bayb  Camotes Is. Cabalian
Cuyo Is.  Miagao  Bogo  8088  Danao  Maasin  Dinagat
Dumaran  Cuyo  San Carlos  Cebu  Dapa  Siargao
Bartan  Dumaran  Piedra Blanca I.  Guimaras  Talibon  Bohol  Surigao  Bucas Grande
5225  Barbacan  Panay Gulf  Cebu  Tagbilaran  Dinagat  Cauit Pt
Cauayan  Argao  Guindulman
PALAWAN  Puerto Princesa  NEGROS  Bais
Aborlan  Cayagan Is.  Tolong  Labonga  Lanuza
Siquior  Lianga
Eran  Tubbataha Reefs  Siaton  Siquior Sea  Camiguin  Hinatuan
6785  Mindanao Sea  Talisayan  Butuan  Gingoog
Brooke's Pt  Dapitan  Camiguin  Lingig
Cauipan  Mt Dapiak  Oroquieta  Cagayan  Cateel
SULU  8620  Misamis  Iligan  Mailag
Bugsuk  Sindangan  Dansalan  Baganga
Balabac  Kabasalan  L. Lanao  Ragang Volcano  MINDANAO  Caraga
Balabac  SEA  9236  Cotabato  Davao  Manay
Balabac Strait  Malabang  Mati
Banguey  Zamboanga  Moro Gulf  Buluan  Apo Volcano  Samal  Lupon
Cayagan Sulu  Buluan  Santa Cruz  9690  Davao Gulf  Surup
Pilas  Lamitan  Lebac  C. San Augustin
Kinabalu  Maluso  Basilan  Sebu  Buayan
13455  Pangutaran Group  Jolo  Samales Group  Luan  Caburan
Paranga  Jolo  Kling  Glan
NORTH BORNEO  Tapul Group  Tinaca Pt  Batulaki
C. Unsang  Tawitawi  CELEBES SEA  Sarangani Is.
Sulu Archipelago
Balimbing
Sibutu

western parts and where shifting cultivation is practised, fires have been responsible for areas of bamboo and coarse grasses.

**Land Tenure and Farming:** About one fifth of the total area is farmed in some 1,700,000 farm units. Only about 40 per cent of the 15,000,000 acres of farmland is worked by owner farmers and more than half the farms are less than five acres in size. The chief food crop is padi or wet rice, which occupies 40 per cent of cultivated land. It is grown on the flats and on terraces (mainly in northern Luzon). Other crops are maize (chiefly in Cebu), sweet potatoes, bananas, marioc, beans, groundnuts and tropical fruits.

The main export crops are coconuts (23 per cent of cultivated land), hemp, sugar and tobacco, grown by small farmers and on plantations. The Philippines lead the world in exports of copra and coconut oil. Chief domestic animals are pigs, water buffalo, cattle, goats, horses, sheep and chickens. Fish is important in the diet, especially for coastal people.

**Exports:**              **1965**

|  | Value in Pesos |
|---|---|
| Coconuts (copra, oil, etc.) | 1,047,000,000 |
| Sugar and Sugar Preparation | 607,000,000 |
| Minerals | 233,000,000 |
| Timber and Plywood | 664,000,000 |
| Hemp (abaca) and Textile Fibre | 118,000,000 |

**Industry:** Local handicrafts of weaving, textiles, woodcarving and metalwork are practised all over the islands.

Mining of gold, silver, iron, chromium, manganese and copper is important. There is coal of low quality. Manufacturing is concerned mainly with textiles, cement, coconut oil milling, rice milling, tobacco manufacture, sugar milling, drinks, soaps, furniture and other domestic products. There is considerable use of hydro-electric power.

**Towns:** Manila (1,700,000) is the largest city and chief port, being on the main shipping routes, but Quezon City (390,000) just north-east of Manila, is the capital. Cebu (167,000) in the Visayan Islands is the second most important port. Davao (228,000) is the centre of the hemp industry in Mindanao. There are several other large towns.

**Communications:** There are almost 20,000 miles of roads but these are still inadequate especially in Palawan, Mindoro and Mindanao. Railways in Luzon and Panay are used chiefly for carrying rice, sugar and timber. Inter-island transport is well catered for by ships, launches, small boats and aircraft. Daily air services link Manila to the rest of the world. Towns are well supplied with telephone, radio and television services. Nearly 500 newspapers and periodicals are published.

**Special Features:**
1. The Philippines are on the edge of the Pacific and the Orient and are culturally akin to South-east Asia.
2. The University of Santo Tomas in Manila was founded in 1611.

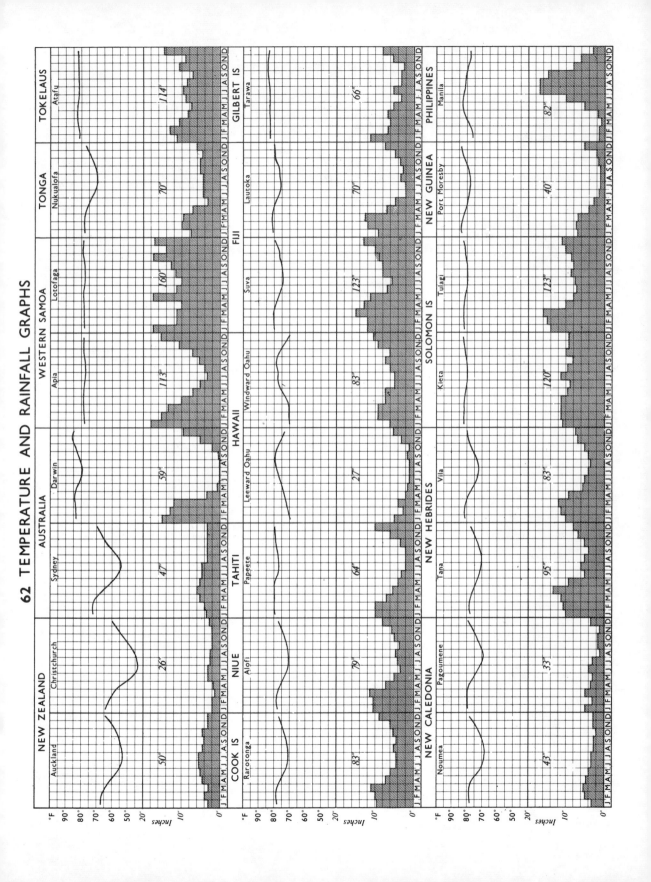

# 62 TEMPERATURE AND RAINFALL GRAPHS

# INDEX TO MAPS
Bold figures indicate map numbers